CHRISTIAN THEOLOGY TODAY

CHRISTIAN THEOLOGY TODAY

by
S. W. SYKES

MOWBRAYS
LONDON & OXFORD

© *S. W. Sykes, 1971*

Printed in Great Britain by
Alden & Mowbray Ltd at the Alden Press, Oxford

SBN 264 64553 7 (boards)

SBN 264 64552 9 (paper)

First published in 1971

CONTENTS

PREFACE

I was invited to write this work for the benefit of the 'man in the street', or at least for such of them as want to understand the changing world in which they live. My willingness to write to this specification was based solely on the belief that one of the important responsibilities of academic theologians is to explain as clearly as they can what is going on in their subject as a whole. In many ways it is easier to be more specialised, and to cover one's tracks with detail, complications and footnotes. But here my brief was to write a few things clearly. The book is written, therefore, for those who want to know something about a subject to which they may not previously have given much attention. A highly select bibliography is appended to entice the interested reader further.

But what is theology? Politicians commonly use the word 'theology' for what they wish to depict as the arbitrary and doctrinaire views of their opponents. This would scarcely be an appropriate use of the word unless it were true that theologians have disastrously failed to communicate a sense that their work engages with the real world in a valuable way. Can Christian theology recover the initiative from those who present it as a series of alternately defensive or frantically *avant-garde* reactions to a hostile environment? I believe this depends on the extent to which a clear position emerges in which Christian faith is recognisably continuous with the past and yet open to the future. The delineation, however, of such a position cannot be achieved by the clouding of difficult issues with pious phraseology. Only radical thought about what it is to be a Christian will be sufficient for this task, to which this book is offered as an introduction.

I wish most gratefully to acknowledge help from many sources; Dr D. L. Frost, Mr R. J. Hinton and Miss C. Nilakantan who read the proofs; the Rev. D. W. Hardy, the Rev. R. Morgan, Dr R. W. A. MacKinney and Mr R. Ambler who made suggestions about the bibliography. Were I to make a dedication of the book it would be to the memory of my former Supervisor and Director of Studies, the Rev. Canon J. S. Bezzant (1897–1967). But it is precisely my still so fresh and vivid memory of him, which, for reasons which his pupils will recognise, rules out the gesture.

INTRODUCTION

THIS is a short work of a rather peculiar character. Its aim is to put the reader in possession of what the author believes to be the most important aspects of the conditions under which theology is done today. Theology is one of a number of important subjects which are *too* important to be left to the experts. It is an enterprise which requires the critical attention of both experts in other fields and the ordinary public. This work is therefore for both; and I would like these readers to be quite clear about what I am, and what I am not, attempting to do.

In the first place a certain amount of historical placing of contemporary theology is necessary—not, I hope, in the rather dull manner of an historical review, but by continuous reference to those aspects of our attitude towards the world which have strongly influenced modern theologians. In particular I attach great importance to the fact that while most of the publicly remembered elements of theology stem from an essentially pre-critical past (the Scriptures themselves, the creeds and almost all the hymns of the Christian Church), it is a presupposition of all modern theology that it takes place in a most rigorously critical (by which one does not mean sceptical) environment. Because of this one is constantly obliged to stress the very great difference to the theological enterprise that living in the modern age implies. Looked at from our present perspective we can see how much stems from the late seventeenth and early eighteenth centuries in that truly momentous stage of human thought and enterprise which we call the enlightenment. In a sense this little book might be described as an attempt to assess how much difference to theology the enlightenment made and is still making.

Secondly, on the other hand, I am trying a more positive line (and, some would say, a more foolhardy one) in trying to establish some of the characteristics which the theology of the future will need to exhibit if it is to be at the same time true to itself, true to its new environment, and true. Here I have two points which I want to establish: First, that theology must be *pluriform*, rather than uniform, and that it must learn not merely to tolerate this condition as something regrettable but recognise it as a necessary condition of its essential activity; and secondly, that theology requires a new understanding of the essence of Christianity if it is ever to attempt to resolve its doctrinal disagreements. Pursuit of this latter point has led me to try to give an account of the *character or spirit of Christ* as that which, at all costs, theology must faithfully try to exhibit.

Thus, thirdly, there will inevitably be an element—but only an element—of reassessment of some Christian doctrines. It is *not* the function of this book to 'restate Christian belief for today', although inevitably the author's own wrestling with the major themes of doctrine have resulted in some doctrinal statements. The reason for the lack of material is a self-imposed limitation. It is not that I believe that this is no time for such restatement—that was a shibboleth of the 'sixties—nor that such restatement is beyond the powers of a single individual. (The suggestion that a committee can write doctrine for today is surely ludicrous). The stating of Christian doctrine for today remains a highly personal task for a very few well-qualified and endowed individuals. But our expectations of them, if my contentions about pluriformity are correct, must be neither on the scale nor to the pattern of Aquinas'

Summa or even Tillich's *Systematic Theology*. A future generation will, I believe, find elements of Karl Barth's dogmatic method (if neither his length nor his basis) far more a model for theological writing than either of these systematic treatises.

Yet it is assuredly with the giants of theology that we must wrestle. Their mistakes, when they make them, are of course gigantic; and their lesser disciples have the uncanny knack of perpetuating and institutionalising those parts of them which apparently provide the most cover for their own intellectual deficiencies. For this reason I am not keen to do more than hint at a possible way in which theologies will need to be written in the coming years. The reader will not find a satisfactory treatment of the subject of the divinity of Christ, the atonement or the doctrine of the last things. For these he will have to look elsewhere. Should he, however, have read this book first he may be in a better position to judge why modern theologians write in the way they do, and perhaps also to begin to make an estimate of their success.

S. W. SYKES

I

LIBERALISM IN THEOLOGY

I BELIEVE it is imperative to come straight to the point.

Christians believe that in the whole event of Jesus Christ they have been shown something of unparallelled importance about God. An all-embracing interpretation of the significance of that event for nature and for history was developed over the ages in Christian theology. The authority for that theology, the basis on which it was built up, was a complex interrelation and interaction of the documents of the early Church and its ancient traditions, validated by the Spirit-guided decisions of the apostles' direct descendants, the bishops. Although the Protestant reformers contradicted the claims of the Pope to represent those decisions and tried to undermine the whole appeal to tradition, on two important matters they agreed with Roman Catholics; first, that infallible authority for the content of Christian theology really existed, and, secondly, that many important doctrines, for example relating to the Trinity or the person of Christ, had been correctly formulated in the early Church and handed on to their times.

By contrast, an increasing number of Christian theologians from the seventeenth century onwards have lost either or both of these shared convictions. These theologians have embraced Liberalism in theology, and it is with this phenomenon that everyone who wishes to consider theology today must somehow come to grips.

From the seventeenth century Liberalism has emerged in one form or another, and has been recognised by a variety of names: Latitudinarian, Broad Church (as distinct from both High and Low Church), Liberal Protestant, Liberal Catholic, Liberal Evangelical, Modernist and, more recently, Radical, have all had their vogue. Because the precise content of these terms has often depended upon a contemporary situation in secular philosophy or ecclesiastical politics, it is impossible to say concretely what is common to them. At the same time it is possible to offer a general definition of liberalism in theology by which all these diverse terms can be recognised to be identifiably 'liberal'. Liberalism in theology is that mood or cast of mind which is prepared to accept that some discovery of reason may count *against* the authority of a traditional affirmation in the body of Christian theology. One is a theological liberal if one allows autonomously functioning reason to supply arguments against traditional belief and if one's reformulation of Christian belief provides evidence that one has ceased to believe what has been traditionally believed by Christians.

For many Protestant Christians the most momentous step of theological liberalism is taken when they deny the traditionally accepted belief in the inerrancy of Scripture. The non-liberal solution to the many apparent contradictions which have been noticed from the earliest times is well expressed by Augustine (writing about AD 397):

> If we are perplexed by an apparent contradiction in scripture, it is not permissible to say, the author of this book is mistaken; instead, the manuscript is faulty, or the translation is wrong, or you have not understood. . . . We are bound to receive as true whatever the canon shows to have been said by even one prophet or apostle or evangelist.*

The liberal cast of mind would, on the other hand, be prepared to weigh the relevant evidence. In theology it might well be the

* Contra Faustum Manichaeum 11,5.

case that this task is well nigh impossible because he is attempting to weigh things which are strictly incomparable. He might, for example, have to set the rationally argued case against any individual miraculous event, with proper allowance for transmission of the text as Augustine insists, against his estimate of the claims made for the supernatural power of the agent. The result of such weighing of evidence is likely to be both provisional and cautious. His final verdict may be in favour of the reliability of the document or it may be against, but it will not be *in principle* favourable, nor will he be unprepared to reopen the question in the light of new evidence.

Similarly, for many Roman Catholics the most momentous step may be the acknowledgment that one aspect or another of the Church's solemnly defined tradition is simply wrong when viewed in the light of some fact or discovery. The difficult decision is whether to cross the boundary between saying that a traditional doctrine needs to be *re-interpreted* in the light of modern knowledge, and saying that it needs to be *repudiated* in the light of that knowledge. For there comes a time in the process of re-interpretation when a fresh look at the original sources reveals that one has in effect adopted a new standpoint. In this case it is mere verbal deception to speak of 're-interpretation'.

As so defined liberalism is an extremely common cast of mind in theology, and it may well characterise even those who would be inclined to refer to themselves as 'conservative'. But even such 'conservatives' ought to be prepared to recognise how much divides them from the mental outlook of those who, like Augustine, would be unprepared to believe that anything reported in the Bible could be less than inerrant, or who, like many Roman Catholics in past centuries, could bring themselves to doubt or to qualify what the Pope had proclaimed to be infallible truth. Indeed particularly those of a conservative cast of mind, who wish to retain all that is valuable from the past, need to beware of overlooking how our fundamental attitudes have changed in this matter of the authority of traditional Christianity. A genuine revolution has taken place; certainly, not without equally genuine continuity with the past, but with very far-reaching results for theological work.

The rest of this chapter will consist in a substantiation of the assertion that something fundamental happened to theology when liberalism in theology became a genuine possibility. It is as well to review the evidence with great care, since the assertion is all too commonly presented as an assumption and nearly as commonly attacked as a misunderstanding. It is the attitude to liberalism which, in fact, creates the great divide in the contemporary Christian Church. And unless one is clear precisely what is and is not involved in it, it will be unclear how great a difference the liberal attitude makes.

It will at once be noticed that the rise of liberalism coincides with the beginnings in the seventeenth century of modern scientific inquiry. But whether this 'coincidence' can be developed to make either one the cause of the other is at least debatable. Popularly, of course, it is felt that 'science disproves the Bible'. The notorious clash in 1860 between the Tractarian Bishop of Oxford, Samuel Wilberforce, and the young scientist, T. H. Huxley, at a meeting of the British Association remains for many a paradigm of the Church's defensive attitude faced with the advancing tide of scientific knowledge. The occasion of disagreement was Darwin's *Origin of Species*, which even some eminent scientists regarded as the work of a pretentious amateur. But in the debate Huxley was victorious over the attempted ridicule of the Bishop.* Darwinism gained increasing acceptance and it became widely believed that the

* An excellent account of the event exists in C. E. Raven, *Science, Religion and the Future* (Cambridge, 1943), ch. 3.

book badly undercut the Christian theological position. The dilemma was well put by an Anglican bishop in 1944 when describing the effect of *The Origin of Species* upon his father, a distinguished doctor brought up in a conventionally religious home:

> This [book] wrecked his faith, chiefly because it was not reconcilable with the biblical account of creation, and as the biblical revelation hung together and was all of one piece, if part of it fell out, the rest would fall out too. If Adam never existed, he did not sin; if he did not sin; man was not fallen; there was therefore no need for Christ to come. If the Bible was wrong in science, how could we be sure it was right in theology?*

This, the immediate effect, was not the only effect of the book, as will be seen. But it illustrates the statement 'science disproves the Bible', which is still widely accepted as the major objection to continuing to believe the Christian faith.

To get at the origins of this view, we have naturally to go much further back into the history of science, and to observe with greater care precisely what elements of 'science' had a damaging effect on the structure of Christian belief. The usual way of writing the story of the 'Warfare of Science with Theology'—the title of a two-volume history published in America in 1896—is to trace the triumphant progress of observation over the blind dogmatism of the middle ages, citing the case of the vindication of Galileo (1564–1642) as a typical example. A more recent writer, a theoretical physicist and philosopher of science, has placed the matter on its head:

> The late middle ages are in no way dark ages, they are a time of high culture, bristling with intellectual energy. They adopted Aristotle because of his concern with reality. But the main weakness of Aristotle was that he was too empirical. Therefore he could not achieve a mathematical theory of nature. Galileo

* S. Leeson, *Christian Education* (London, 1947), pp. 97–8.

took his great step in daring to describe the world as we do not experience it.*

The popular reputation of the Church as an opponent of scientific progress is not, of course, without foundation, and the judgement by the Congregation of the Inquisition upon Galileo for speculations contrary to Holy Scripture is a particularly striking confrontation. But it is not the whole story, nor is it even typical.

The real position is more complicated, and concerns not merely particular scientific discoveries but a whole attitude towards the world. As an eminent English theologian wrote towards the end of the nineteenth century, 'Great scientific discoveries, like the heliocentric astronomy, are not merely new facts to be assimilated; they involve new ways of looking at things'.†

In relation to scientific discovery what ultimately mattered to the medieval Church was far less the challenge to particular items of traditional teaching. These challenges we may regard as symptomatic of a deeper change of attitude towards the patronage and authority of the Church; and in this respect what happened to medieval Christendom at the Reformation and during the Thirty Years War (1618–48) is still more important for the attitude of educated men towards the authority of the Church. The sight of Western Christendom deeply and bloodily divided in religion was an object lesson not lost on those who were beginning to claim for themselves the freedom to inquire about any subject whatsoever. In these early centuries the basis of the kind of scepticism that existed, for example, in the essays of Montaigne (1533–92), was the humane moderation of ancient philosophy and morals, which

* C. F. von Weizsäcker, *The Relevance of Science* (London, 1964), p. 104.
† J. R. Illingworth in *Lux Mundi*, Essay V,' The Incarnation and Development' (London, 1859), p. 182.

might be favourably contrasted with the frenzied fanaticism of the wagers of religious war. The freedom to value the sanity of non-Christian rational thought is no innovation in the history of Christianity, but an important rediscovery nevertheless. The feeling was abroad that the last word was not being spoken by the Church, and that the moral authority of an already disunited body was open to question. In the end the development of spheres of thought and inquiry potentially independent of the overarching of the Christian world view merely reinforced the already well-learnt lesson of human limitation and fallibility in matters of religion.

The coincidence of war between Protestant and Catholic with important and prestigious developments in scientific fields is clearest during the Thirty Years War. In 1619 Johannes Kepler (1571–1630), a devout Lutheran and a mathematical genius, published his *Harmonices Mundi*, in which he enunciated the third of his three laws governing the movement of the planets. William Harvey (1578–1658), an English physician who had studied at Padua, produced in 1628 a revolutionary work on the circulation of the blood. In 1632 Galileo Galilei published his famous *Dialogues*, an attack on Ptolemaic astronomical theory which brought down the wrath of the Inquisition upon his head. Similarly in England the twenty years of Civil War, Commonwealth and Restoration witnessed the beginnings of that great flowering of scientific interest stimulated by Francis Bacon (1561–1626) and continued by Robert Boyle (1627–91), Robert Hooke (1635–1703) and Isaac Newton (1642–1727).

Also of importance was the growth of a philosophical vocabulary relatively independent of the Latin terminology of scholasticism. René Descartes (1596–1650) wrote his important *Discourse on Method* (1637) in French. A philosopher who was fascinated by mathematics, he tried to construct for philosophy and physical science a method of argument based upon simple, fundamental and indubitable truths. He was a Catholic and found no inconsistency between his work and the traditional faith. But the effect of his writing was further to free philosophy from the categories and methods of traditional thought, and to demonstrate that progress in the understanding of experience and reality might be made irrespective of the religious belief of the enquirer.

I have emphasised above the importance of the decline in authority of the Church for the new independence of philosophical and scientific investigation. But that by itself is by no means the whole story. For there were genuine changes taking place in man's attitude to the world as a result of the work of the scientists and philosophers. In particular the use of mathematical and mechanical explanations of the natural order was leading to a new understanding of the relations of God and the world. Though God may still be said to deal with man, as a living soul, exactly as he was always thought to deal with him, namely directly, God's relation to physical nature was now conceived on the analogy of an inventor and a machine. Newton, for example, a convinced if not orthodox Christian, strongly argued the existence of God from the order of the universe, which demonstrates a 'cause not blind or fortuitous, but very well skilled in mechanics and geometry'.* In such a well-ordered universe, God might appear to be dangerously without present employment. Again for Newton this need was met by various irregularities to be corrected and by the sustaining of the whole in harmony. Thus God was not quite eliminated from a universe which was being explained in mechanical terms. But an important change had taken place in which the *nature* of God's activity in the world was becoming problematic to men of science. From Francis Bacon (1561–1626) onwards we find lay scientists and philosophers speculating about the relative claims of reason and faith

* I. Newton, *Opera*, IV, 429 ff.

in relation to knowledge of the world. Thus Bacon distinguishes firmly; 'all knowledge proceeds from a twofold source—either from divine inspiration or external sense'.* From external sense, the sphere of philosophy, we may indeed learn much about God's nature and attributes; but it is not safe to use reason in revealed religion, except in making deductions from basic principles. While he believed that scientific inquiry supported religious faith in a general way he would have nothing to do with those who tried to confirm the truth of the Christian religion by the authority of science or philosophy.† Thus an important, but ultimately dangerous wedge began to be driven between religion and science, faith and reason. Those who believed that God's existence, nature and activity might be inferred from physical nature found themselves positing a Deity strangely different from the God of the Old and New Testaments. In order to preserve the absolute sanctity of faith and the authority of Scripture the kind of reason being used so fruitfully in the sphere of science and philosophy was in danger of being denied entrance to religion.

Since the seventeenth century this has remained alive in various guises as a common view of reason and religion, sometimes strangely shared by those who want desperately to defend traditional religion and by those who want, no less eagerly, to attack it. But what are the respective rôles of reason and faith in religion? Here in the very beginning of the seventeenth century we begin to see the outlines of the problem of liberalism in theology.

The problem as I defined it earlier was that an impression was given by advancing scientific knowledge that the Bible was

* *Proficience and Advancement of Learning*, III, 1.
† There is an important distinction here between the *general* truths of religion, and the special revelation of God in Christ. For Bacon philosophy and science can have nothing to do with the latter, which belongs solely to the realm of faith.

disproved. The precise substance behind this impression was that science began to reveal things about the world and man which were previously unknown; which were unknown, that is, to those who formulated the content of Christian theology in its early formative years. The result was twofold; in the first place, conflicts and encounters, such as that between Galileo and the Inquisition, became a genuine possibility—the Church teaching views about the world which are factually incorrect—and, secondly and more importantly, the Church no longer remained in sole control of the development of the Christian view of the world, as independent disciplines began to contribute new knowledge about the world and man. This second result is thus a double revolution. No longer does Christian theology supply, as it did in the middle ages, the sole interpretive framework for all reality, nor can it any longer operate in a sovereign and independent way.

Even today it is over the independence of theology that the issue of liberalism becomes particularly controversial and crucial. As our picture of the world and man changes with our greatly increased knowledge and control of our environment, aspects of the biblical and medieval world become very strange and unfamiliar. Our attitudes to everyday things like the weather, natural disasters or health and disease have changed vastly; so have our understanding of man's place in the universe and our expectations of how life will treat us. The religious writing of past centuries sometimes requires a real effort of historical imagination to appreciate. In particular, scepticism about tales of the supernatural has become the almost instinctive response of the great majority of Western society.

These are points which have often been made, and sometimes overstressed. We have on occasion been over-confident about the extent to which we understand our world and control it; often enough we have overlooked the very considerable elements of continuity between our times and those of our ancestors. By our often blind obeisance to novelty, we have created a generation who know nothing of the past of the human race, and wish to remain ignorant. No one reading Aristophanes' plays or Ovid's love poetry in a lively translation could doubt the elements of continuity in relation to at least some human characteristics.

The question not unnaturally arises, then, whether what one might tentatively call one's 'religious consciousness' is not also an invariable constant, persisting unchanged from era to era. To what extent is it really *necessary* to alter the traditional concepts of Christian faith to bring them into keeping with modern thought? As we saw, Bacon, at the beginning of the seventeenth century, hoped to keep religion *unchanged* by distinguishing sharply between what may be known by divine inspiration and what may be known by external sense. But reason did not tolerate this distinction for long. Soon the documents and dogmas of Christianity were subjected to historical, logical and moral scrutiny. The conclusion that they contained human, fallible elements became a tolerable position, first in Protestantism and eventually also in Catholicism. But even if one grants that dogmas of infallibility are exaggerated, is it still not possible to identify and define the eternal verities of the Christian religion—those things which have been believed down the ages and remain the solid foundation of true believing and living?

I propose to tackle the problem of a persisting 'essence' of Christianity in a later chapter, after we have taken a look at some of the particular interests of theology today. For the time being, two points of a rather negative kind have to be mentioned in order to illustrate the rather great difficulty of thinking of the 'eternal verities' in any absolute manner. The first consideration concerns the problem of vocabulary. Suppose one wanted to answer that the Christian religion had been or could be defined for all time in certain words, we would immediately be faced with the fact that, even if words do not change, meanings frequently do. We would further be faced with the difficulty of translating the words from one language to another. Could we be certain that, in so doing, we would be translating the same meaning? A very useful example is the statement in the Apostle's Creed that Christ was 'of one substance with the Father'. It is certain that the Greek word 'of one substance' meant a good many different things to those who first accepted it as expressing part of the Christian faith in AD 325. It is likewise true that a large number of Protestant theologians have thought that the word does not convey much to the minds of modern men, and have tried to translate the term into something with more contemporary meaning. Furthermore, since it is not a biblical term they differ among themselves even as to whether the 'idea behind the term' is a necessary part of the Christian faith. The problem of vocabulary is thus twofold; which words in which language comprise the expression of the content of Christian belief? and, how does one know in translating from one language to another, or from one idiom to another in the same language, that one has genuinely conveyed that content? The problem of vocabulary is the problem of conveying meaning by means of words. In being conveyed by speech the 'eternal verities' of the Christian faith are exposed to the possibility of distortion and ambiguities which cannot be overlooked.

The second problem with hoping to preserve 'eternal verities' is still more fundamental. It is the fact that Christian theology is one in which the meaning of every word begins from some familiar human situation and is then extended transcendentally.

> God loved the world so much that he gave his only Son, that everyone who has faith in him may not die but have eternal life (John 3.16, NEB).

'Love', 'die' and 'life' are all words of everyday speech, evoking ordinary human situations. But their meaning in the context of the gospel of John is stretched beyond that context to another realm, the realm or kingdom of God, which, according to John, gives the true understanding of life.

If Christian theology is concerned with the true understanding of life, then it is bound to be affected by changes in our understanding of the natural conditions of life. In this respect, there have been two particularly important changes as a result first of Darwin, and subsequently of Freud. Man is now obliged to see himself not simply as a special creation, uniquely endowed with capacities of rationality, but as continuous with the rest of nature and substantially at the mercy of non-rational forces. The work of Darwin and Freud has individually had a most disturbing effect on traditional Christianity; Darwin, in as much as no room seems to be made for a Fall at some point of time, and Freud, by the insecurity and uncertainty he introduced into the very heart of most fundamentally held convictions of man. But when combined with the findings of neurophysiological research a picture emerges of man as an animal with particular urges and drives, whose evolution has reached the stage of his possessing self-awareness but whose own fundamental mechanisms he may one day be able to understand and control.

In this picture there appears to be no room for the spiritual capacities of soul, no reason to believe that man survives his death, and little place for freedom of will. Thus, though in some respects the newer ideas of the non-rationality of many of man's basic urges come as no surprise to those who have believed in the Fall, the new understanding of man poses considerable difficulties for the traditional Christian understanding of life. Even the words we mentioned are not unaffected. The point we are making is that because Christian theology is about the life of man, its origin and purpose, his destiny and his salvation, it is not possible for it to remain unaffected by what scientists may claim to be true about man's natural condition. This is not to say that the Christian view of man is superseded by the scientific view of man, precisely because the Christian has something further to say when the scientist has stopped speaking of the natural conditions of life. But what the Christian cannot do is to ignore the scientist, even if that were any longer possible now that scientific knowledge is so widely disseminated. In as much as the 'eternal verities' were formulated at a time when such knowledge was not available, their proclamation in the contemporary world is bound to be influenced by it. The extent of the influence remains a further question; the history of the last 300 years of theology has numerous examples of theologians who jumped on the bandwaggon of the latest scientific hypothesis only to find themselves in the knacker's yard. This is a subject which receives attention in the next chapter. But there can be no question but that the new knowledge upsets the deceptive simplicity of talk about 'eternal verities'.

2

THE VALIDITY OF CONSERVATISM

THE CHURCH has every reason to be conservative. I say this in conscious reaction against the cries for radical reform heard from many sides. But what is 'the Church'? This is a question which is not always made clear. In the preface to *Honest to God*, Dr J. A. T. Robinson wrote:

> When we consider the distance we have all moved since then [a hundred years ago], we can see that almost everything said from within the Church at the time proved too conservative.*

But if there is no guarantee that 'the Church' will come to the right solution of every difficulty, we cannot by an inversion of the same principle suppose that 'the Church' will inevitably, and on every question, be wrong. It is useless in any given controversy to distinguish first a conservative then a radical view point and unhesitatingly, and without further reflection, identify oneself with the radical view. Views are neither right nor wrong by being identified as radical or as conservative. And if Dr Robinson can point to conservative standpoints taken by 'the Church' in the past, one would have no difficulty in pointing to radical views, which are no less untenable today

* pp. 9-10. I believe it necessary to remind English readers that the Church of England in 1860 was approximately 50 years behind German theological opinion. Many English controversies were aggravated by the fact that German scholarship had been studiously ignored or despised, in a way which is not without example even today.

and which, if 'the Church' had capitulated to them, would have had to be subsequently repudiated.*

The real problem here is what constitutes the judgement of 'the Church'. As an example we may take (with Dr Robinson) the Colenso controversy of 100 years ago. Unquestionably it is true that the bishops of the Church of England took the part of traditional orthodoxy. Bishop Colenso of Natal attacked in 1862 the Mosaic authorship of the Pentateuch and the doctrine of the eternal punishment of the damned. Forty-one bishops urged him to resign and a rival 'orthodox' bishop was consecrated in Natal. But 'the Church' was divided in its attitude; in particular two eminent men supported Colenso, Bishop Thirwall of St David's, intellectually the most powerful bishop on the bench, and A. P. Stanley, Dean of Westminster. The sentence of deposition and excommunication passed by the Archbishop of Capetown was declared null and void by the Judicial Committee of the Privy Council and the rival Bishop of Natal was consecrated in Cape Town without a mandate from the Crown.

Colenso certainly enjoyed the popular reputation of a martyr for liberal thought, and undoubtedly a man who was supported publicly by theologians of the calibre of Thirwall and Stanley was no fool. But the ultimate verdict on Colenso is by no means an unqualified crown of martyrdom. F. D. Maurice (1805–72), who has the reputation for being the most considerable Anglican theologian of the period and who was himself hounded out of his chair at King's College, London, in 1854 for attacking the popular view of the 'eternity' of punishment for the damned, thought that Colenso's attitude to the Old Testament was pedantic and boorish. 'His idea of

* Cf. for example, his own (conservative) attitude to the Fourth Gospel as compared with that of F. C. Baur (1792–1860), in 'The New Look on the Fourth Gospel', *The Gospels Reconsidered* (Oxford, 1960), by K. Aland *et al.*

history is that it is a branch of arithmetic.'* If Colenso was right in some things, he was certainly wrong in others. It is altogether an oversimplification to dismiss the judgement of 'the Church' as both conservative and wrong. The examination of this episode encourages us to adopt a more thoroughly critical attitude towards the reputation of those who have recently received often posthumous medals for gallantry in the face of official persecution by 'the Church'.

But the more fundamental question remains whether we can simply identify the reaction of the bench of bishops with the judgement of 'the Church', even of the Church of England. Two contradictory and equally commonsense answers suggest themselves. The bishops are clearly the leaders of the Church, chosen for their abilities of many kinds. As far at least as the Church of England is concerned no better body exists by which the judgement of 'the Church' is to be gauged. But on the other hand, the very eminence of the bishops prevents them from being representative of 'the Church', in 1870 perhaps even more than 1970. We cannot do more, it would seem, than regard the bishops' views as one element in the judgement of 'the Church'.

In view of this apparent conflict of commonsense answers, we had better ask more carefully about the word, 'Church'. In its singular use with the definite article, 'the Church' is a theological idea, rather than a clear empirical reality. Admittedly there are those who claim that the visible Church consists solely of the members of one body, be that body Roman Catholic, Eastern Orthodox or Jehovah's Witnesses. But even those members of these bodies who make such a claim admit that the term 'the Church' also includes those who have died in the true faith and form 'the Church in heaven'. There

* Quoted by A. O. J. Cockshut in *Anglican Attitudes* (London, 1959), p. 94. Chapter 5 of this book is a lively account of the issues involved.

would, of course, be many other Christians who would argue that, now that the Church has become so divided, there is no way of determining what 'the Church' is empirically; and some would add that there may be a 'latent Church' among those who do not in any way formally profess the title Christian.* On this view the idea of the judgement of 'the Church' becomes exceedingly problematic. In what way, if at all, can such a diffuse body be expected to render a judgement on any subject whatsoever?

The fact of the matter is that the ambiguity in the term 'the Church' is the source of most of this confusion. In the same breath it is quite possible to curse 'the Church', meaning its officials and formal gatherings, and to bless 'the Church', meaning the body of Christians from which one derives strength and through which the grace of Christ is made available to us. A sermon on 'the Church' can as easily be an ecstatic utterance concerning the mystery of the body of Christ as a robust denunciation of hypocritical officialdom.

This confusion ought, however, not to be prolonged. To the question, What do you mean by 'the Church' in the sentence 'the Church has every reason to be conservative'?, we reply: Those to whom is committed the task of preserving the witness of a body of Christians to the truth of the gospel, in other words, a given Church's leadership. If it is true that the leadership may with good reason be conservative in attitude, this is not intended to prejudice the issue of the attitude of each and every member of that Church. Nor is it intended to apply to political and social questions, which may raise very different sorts of issues in morality. The assertion that 'the Church' (in the sense defined) has every reason to be conservative must be understood to mean that its leadership must be expected to be cautious in matters which concern the witness of Christians

* See, for example, Paul Tillich in his *Systematic Theology*, III London, 1964), pp. 162 ff.

to the truth of the Gospel—in a word, we cannot expect Church leadership to be theologically radical.

In fact the leaders of the Church may not be theologians at all. In quite a similar way any given Chancellor of the Exchequer may not be an economist. The statements and decisions which bishops or chancellors may have to make must certainly take into account the views of the experts, and they must certainly be subject to the experts' criticisms. But in as much as they have to commend themselves to a very much wider circle of people than experts in theology or economics, the range of considerations brought to bear may well be very much wider than those which the expert would consider strictly relevant. Of course, in both cases questions of fact and truth are involved, to which expert and non-expert are alike subject. But the point remains; the functions of a theologian and of a Church leader are not identical. Theology, which has in a happy phrase been described as 'the servant of the Church', may not necessarily be a good master.

It may seem that having vigorously argued in the previous chapter for the inevitability of liberalism in theology we are now engaged in retracting all that was there said by starting to defend conservatism. To commend change in one chapter and caution in another is certainly to invite the charge of inconsistency; and in meeting this charge, the position one wants to defend is certainly *not* the desirability of slow change. Instead, I wish to offer the concept of the necessary *pluriformity* of 'the Church'. The inevitable pluriformity of the Church is, indeed, one of the major consequences of liberalism. Up until the liberal revolution in theology, uniformity in Catholicism and Protestantism was pursued in the name of the absolute authority of either the Papacy or of scripture. The liberal critique of these authorities claims to have ended the absolute right of either to be the sole focus of unity in Christendom. If this critique is successful, as the previous chapter believes it to be, the possibility of uniformity in the Church awaits the successful establishment of a new focal point. Until there is such a focal point by reference to which all disputes in theology or Church life may be concluded, we must expect that pluriformity rather than uniformity will be the natural condition of the contemporary Church.

In this respect it is possible that we may resemble the early Church rather more closely than we may at first imagine. For the early Church had neither scriptures nor Church leaders whose judgement was unequivocally binding. The authority of the Old Testament was unquestionable; but in the light of the teaching of Jesus a revolution had taken place in the interpretation of it. Certain parts had been clearly superseded, and there was dispute about the extent of the continuing validity of parts of the law. Further, neither Paul, nor Peter, nor any other of the apostles appears to have occupied from the first the position of supreme arbiter, which was given to the words of Christ himself. The early writings of the New Testament makes stirring appeals for unity, but they do so against a background of pluriformity of both belief and practice. In the New Testament, unity is something hoped for, not a present possession.*

If then the position of the Church is inevitably rather that of a pluriform than of a uniform body, it is a position of which we had better become fully conscious. There are two senses in which the Church is pluriform, and both are important.

(1) *There is pluriformity of function within the Church.* Of this it is easy to write; indeed there is nothing new about it. It was clear to Paul, writing his letters of 1 Corinthians and Romans, that 'the gifts we possess differ as they are allotted to us by God's grace, and must be exercised accordingly' (Rom. 12.6,

---

* It should be noted here that I wish to distinguish between unity and uniformity. See below, p. 33.

NEB, cf. 1 Cor. 12.4–31). He visualises a community in which the members, having different functions to perform, nevertheless, as organs of a single body, co-operate for the common good. The writer of the letter to the Ephesians, whether Paul or not, also sees the diversity of function as an essential part in Christian growth to maturity. The body of the Church depends upon Christ, who is its head; 'bonded and knit together by every constituent joint, the whole frame grows through the due activity of each part, and builds itself up in love' (Eph. 4.16, NEB).

It is, of course, easier to state the doctrine than it is to accept the consequences of it. The history of the Church, up to and including the present day, is full of instances of the eye saying to the hand, 'I do not need you'. Parties in the Church, initially formed to ensure the continuance of a certain tradition of the Church's ministry, have degenerated into self-sufficient cliques with monotonous regularity. Suspicion and intrigue have followed when it appeared that a certain party had gained effective control of the councils of the Church. In such circumstances petty differences and divergent emphases in theology have become magnified in order to justify separation and exclusion. Without denying or diminishing the importance of theological argument, it is nevertheless easy to find instances where theology has been used as the excuse for failing to allow for the possibility of functional pluriformity in the Church.

The problem here is often enough one of temperament. Christ's gifts through the Spirit, which Paul lists in 1 Cor. 12, often enough correspond closely to differences of natural endowment. Wise speech, ability to put the deepest knowledge into words, healing powers, prophecy, distinguishing of spirits, ecstatic utterance and ability to interpret are commonly, though not invariably, the abilities of men with corresponding natural endowments. Thus the gift of wise speech may be seen

C

in men of considerable natural powers of intellect, and so forth. These divergencies of natural gifts have often enough given rise to suspicions and antipathies. The cool-headed man fears rashness and impetuosity; the man of average intellectual ability is suspicious of the academic. When reduplicated inside the Church in the differing functions of evangelism, prophecy, teaching, healing or administration, precisely that kind of futile and wasteful conflict against which Paul expostulates may, indeed frequently has been seen to, take place. There is no protection against it which survives the passing of one generation and the rise of another. It is a lesson which has to be learnt by experience, guided by the wisdom of Paul.

But there is a corollary of functional pluriformity which is not always mentioned. A function in the Church, arising perhaps out of a certain natural endowment, may necessitate or suggest a certain pattern of piety. For example those who are evangelists in the Church may respond to and appreciate a certain pattern of Church worship or of devotional life. In practice, of course, the Evangelical 'party' or 'wing' in the Church exhibits precisely this feature. It is bound together not merely by doctrinal agreements, but also by a pattern of devotion which has marked attractions for men of certain abilities and temperaments. This is by no means to minimise their appropriateness. God's gifts of the spirit are to each one individually; and not unnaturally they result in an individually unique orientation of the personal and devotional life. This is not merely the commonsense teaching of 'one man's meat is another man's poison' or '*chacqun à son gout*', though common sense may be capable of preventing a good deal of wasteful conflict between Christians of differing gifts and patterns of devotion. It is a more basic realisation that within the potential richness of the life lived in the spirit of Christ there are to be expected differences of summons. If God's work is to be done in a world of vastly differing patterns of personal and social life, we must expect men to be called to live in different traditions of piety and devotion. To attempt to conform all Christians to a uniform ideal would be a great mistake and danger.

(ii) *There is pluriformity of belief within the Church.* Of this it is less easy to write since it is manifestly at variance with parts, at least, of the New Testament and with much of Church history. Exhortations to hold fast to one faith, to be of the same mind and to beware of those who alter the tradition of 'sound words' abound in the letters of the New Testament. The fight against Gnostic corruptions* had already begun in the first century and created the Church's consciousness of the necessity for orthodoxy. We must see the early Church's concern for uniformity of teaching against the background of the very real danger of its gospel being swallowed up by alien speculation.

At the same time it is perfectly possible to ask whether the New Testament itself does exhibit *uniformity* of belief. We may question whether the appeals for uniformity are entirely consistent with the slight, but none the less real, divergencies which the New Testament shows in its theology. Certainly one of the most important branches of the study of the New Testament has been comparative accounts of the theologies of Paul and John, of John and the Synoptics, and, most recently, of Mark, Luke and Matthew themselves.

We may further ask the question whether uniformity of *belief* is indeed possible; or if it is possible, whether it is possible to be sure about. One can approach uniformity of belief by establishing uniformity of confession. But even when

* Gnosticism is the name for certain features of a very widespread religious movement in the first and especially second centuries AD. Essentially referring to salvation by gnosis (or knowledge), it tended to develop more or less fantastic theories of secret teachings designed to free the truly spiritual man from the shackles of fleshly existence.

all *say* that they believe the same thing by assenting to the identical form of words, it remains questionable whether all *understand* the same thing by that form of words. For example, in the creed we may say, 'I believe in one God, the Father Almighty, Maker of heaven and earth and of all things visible and invisible'. Whether all understand the same thing by this form of words is open to question, and is indeed only determinable, if at all, by intense and laborious examination. The formidable Bishop Marsh (1757–1839) of Peterborough devised a set of eighty-seven questions for intending clergy in his diocese by which he might detect whether their understanding of the Thirty-Nine Articles of the Church of England was open to an objectionable (Calvinistic) interpretation. The wretched clergy were being quizzed as to the *meaning* of their assent to the Articles; mere assent itself had not established, to the Bishop's satisfaction, a sufficient degree of uniformity of belief.

Where absolute uniformity seems out of the question because of the nature of the subject, it seems then that we are left with degrees of uniformity and of pluriformity. Indeed in this matter it would be better to speak of unity in pluriformity, than to seek to qualify the term uniformity. If there is certain to be at least some degree of pluriformity of belief, it may be misleading to use the word uniformity at all. The word unity, and particularly the phrase 'unity in pluriformity' much more exactly expressed the condition of any united body of Christians engaged in common worship or common activity. And we construe the New Testament more accurately if we think of the appeals for persistence in right teaching as a constant *quest* for unity and coherence in Christ in the *de facto* situation of pluriformity of belief and practice.

Despite this, it would still appear that there is a big difference between on the one hand asserting, and appearing to be content with the assertion, that there is pluriformity of belief in the Church, and on the other considering and acting on the New Testament quest for unity. This difference, I believe, is more apparent than real. Certainly it is true that pluriformity of belief in the Church seems to be its natural condition; but no less certain is the fact that Christians have but one Lord. The appeal for unity in the prayer of John 17, 'that they may be one', is based on the mystical unity of Son and Father— 'as we are one'. 'I in them and thou in me, may they be perfectly one' (NEB, John 17.23). The faith of Christians has one source, and however divergent time, nationality, tradition or temperament may make and have made it, it nevertheless converges at that one point. And in so far as that one point is the sole object of faith, convergence will also be the natural condition of Christian faith. This may be illustrated diagramatically thus:

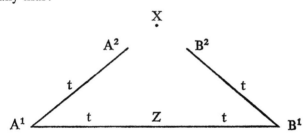

There are two ways in which points A^1 and B^1 may converge on each other. They may choose to attempt agreement by seeking point Z equidistant from each other's separate positions. Or they may choose to set their sights at point X, and in so doing, discover at points A^2 and B^2 that they had noticeably closed the gap between them. The simple point of the diagram is that point Z, though the same distance to travel from points A^1 and B^1, is further from X than the position reached at A^2 and B^2. In terms of the quest for unity between Christians, there are obviously forms of unity conceivable which may actually represent a regression from eventual state of unity in God in Christ, the sole object of Christian faith.

If there are degrees of uniformity, there must obviously also be degrees of unity in pluriformity. To determine the probable extent of pluriformity of belief within the Church we are bound to examine the variables which exist within the Church and may give rise to differences. We have already mentioned the most basic of these, namely the lack of an unambiguous focal point of absolute authority by which disputes in matters of belief may be quickly and finally settled. If there are disputes about the rules of chess, the working of a motor car or the structure of a building, it is a comparatively straightforward business to consult the relevant handbook. The authority of the rules are absolute in the sense that if one proposes a move (say a diagonal move of a castle) which is challenged, it can be finally established that such a move in the game of chess is not allowed. In theology, however, the authorities are various; there are the biblical writings (themselves of unequal weight and containing divergent emphases), the Churches' solemnly defined statements of belief (differently assessed in each Church) and the claims of reason and experience to contribute to the understanding of truth. If a theologian proposes an argument, for example about the divinity of Christ, and this argument is challenged, how is it proposed that the argument shall be settled? By appeal to this gospel or that, or this reconstruction of the gospel or that? by reference to the implications of the teaching of the creeds or this or that Church father? or by some natural light of reason or supernatural gift of spiritual illumination? A more thorough discussion of the differing possibilities must wait until a later chapter, but there is certainly more than one tenable point of view.

To present this situation in its complexity has unquestionably an unnerving effect. An internal combustion engine may seem a very complex thing to a non-engineer, but a man of reasonable intelligence has at least some hope of being able to understand how it works. To be told, however, that from the outset there is difficulty in identifying a final court of appeal to resolve disagreements in theology may make some people abandon the attempt without further ado. It also has another observable effect of making some take refuge in an authority, for no better reason than that it is easier if they have one. But the position being stated here is *not* that there are no authorities in theology, but that no one of them is a final authority in the sense that the rules of chess are final for the game of chess. It is *not* being stated here that the disputes in theology are in principle unresolvable, but that they are difficult to resolve. And so long as they are clearly difficult to resolve it will be necessary to tolerate within the Church a position where some resolve their conflicts one way and some another.

But it is not merely the lack of a clear focal point of authority which creates pluriformity of belief among Christians. Another variable is experience of life. The fact that theology is supposed to have important consequences for one's daily life means that it is liable to have to be reflected in the context of many life-experiences. However, to put the matter only in that way suggests a one-way traffic between theology and life; as though theology were in a position simply to tell as many individuals as fell under its influence how to live their lives. The truth is, rather, that there is two-way exchange of influence; that the way men live their lives today influences the way in which theology may be formulated. The theologian, after all, is a man who lives a fully personal life in a society. He may be married or unmarried, and have particular gifts or failings, interests and blind spots. His work will unquestionably show the mark of these. But it remains true that the life-experience of men is so various that one theologian's theology is unlikely to be able to be applicable to the life-experience of more than a certain proportion of humanity.

A brief illustration will make the point. Many theologians feel the need to 'be in touch' with contemporary culture. Culture, after all, to some degree mirrors the way modern man thinks and assists in shaping his aspirations. If a theologian aspires to address modern man, he may wish to keep himself abreast of the movements in literature, film and theatre and the mass media. At the same time he may wish to reject its influence on himself personally and to regret the debasement and impoverishment of his emotional life that he may consider it entails. He may be sharply critical of its ideals and standards. After a certain exposure to it he may have to face the question of whether the expenditure of time involved was justified by the results, and whether the effect of the influence on himself was even beneficial in the long run to his own theological work. There is no question but that not all individuals possess the same degree of resilience and detachment in facing prolonged exposure to coarseness or brutality. The theologian may therefore have to face the fact that he must necessarily withdraw from deep contact with contemporary culture, and write from a position of relative isolation. What his writing may lose in contemporary appeal it may gain in serenity. While what he says may seem remote to some, to others it will be a source of strength and encouragement.

This is but one illustration of the effect of life-experience upon theological writing. Variables of background, class, nationality, education and even climate may play their part in shaping the character of a theologian's writing, in the choice of problems which he considers need urgently to be tackled and in the depth to which he is able to tackle them. All these variables will give to different theological works in any given generation certainly the appearance, and quite probably the reality of pluriformity of belief. It is not to be expected that a public-school educated, middle-class Englishman will write the theology which underlies the worship and activity of Peruvian Christians. In realising this we have moved at least some distance from our Victorian ancestors; though the great German theologian, Friedrich Schleiermacher (1769–1834), had no greater expectation than that a given theology should be applicable to a given Church at a given time. The next stage is for the contemporary Church to accept pluriformity of belief as a necessary condition of the discipline of theology, and as a sign not of the weakness of its intellectual basis, but of its ability to match the complexity of widely diverging life-experiences.

If the case for pluriformity of belief is established by the above arguments, then it will also follow that Church leaders may be expected to be cautious in matters which concern the witness of Christians to the truth of the gospel. For if it is the case that pluriformity of belief is a necessary condition of theology, then there will always be those who will be inclined to place considerable weight on the value of what has been traditionally believed to be the meaning of the content of the Christian gospel. The function and responsibility of a Church leader is wider than that of a theologian, and while both work under obligation to the truth the presentation of a disputed issue may appear to a Church leader and to a theologian in different lights. Such considerations are manifestly open to abuse. With very little effort, conservatism in theology may become authoritarianism or the attempt to suppress free inquiry. Equally, radical liberalism may become mere iconoclasm for its own sake. Nothing is less edifying than a clash of temperaments between an authoritarian Church leader or body, and an iconoclastic individual. The mere presence of sharp disagreement in the Church is not an infallible sign of profundity of thought.

Conservatism is, however, a tenable approach for the theologian also; *qua* theologian he has no obligation to take radically liberal views. On the contrary the theologian who carefully considers the length of Christian history before his day, the partiality imposed upon him by his own limitations and the nature of his own profession as a Christian may well feel compelled to act in cases of doubt on the principle of the conservation of riches.* For in the course of Christian history aspects of Christian teaching which were neglected in one era have been rediscovered and found to be an invaluable source of enrichment of vision in another. In recent theological history the prime example is that of eschatology, the doctrine of the last things. Frequently relegated in nineteenth-century handbooks of doctrine to an appended chapter, this has now been restored to the very core of theology in a number of works, and is seen to be one of the central themes of Jesus' own teaching. If we had followed the advice of earlier theologians, all this would have been forgotten as 'mythology'.

Further, the variables of temperament and of background which impose so many limitations on the individual theologian's outlook should prevent him from the hasty rejection of aspects of theology which he may consider to be 'irrelevant' or even 'abnormal'. Of nothing is this more true than in speaking of the attitude of mind in which the Christian approaches God. The theologian and the framer of liturgy has to aim to conserve material which will lead forward in Christian life men of widely differing backgrounds and experiences. He must therefore be prepared to restrain the inclination of his own outlook to tyrannise as the only valid criterion of relevance and normality.

Finally, as a Christian himself, the theologian stands in relation to his faith not as a violinist who wishes to make his

* See also Ninian Smart, 'Towards a Systematic Future for Theology' in *Prospect for Theology*, ed. F. G. Healey (London, 1966), pp. 109 ff.

instrument sing songs of his own choosing,* but as a disciple who knows he has to remain teachable if he is himself one day to be able to teach others. The biblical word 'meekness' springs to mind as expressing this attitude of mind towards one's material; and those who have found themselves to be wrong, and have had the courage to admit as much, will know that a meek man, in this sense, is not identical with a man who is prepared to be infinitely imposed upon. Christianity is a faith too thoroughly polemical and self-aware to be ignorant of the fact that one's own limitations can be as great a tyranny as any external constraint. For all these reasons the principle of the conservation of riches ought to commend itself to the theologian as he considers the structure of his work.

* The phrase is Karl Barth's in a somewhat unjust criticism of Schleiermacher, *From Rousseau to Ritschl* (London, 1959), p. 327.

3
PLURIFORMITY AND THE ESSENCE OF CHRISTIANITY

In the chapter on Liberalism I argued that Christianity is bound to accept the fact of change in theology. But, as we saw, change in theology does not imply that the leadership of the Church should implement the instant abandonment of its traditions of belief and worship to match the latest ideas. Change in theology means rather that Christians must learn to live with the continuing possibility of differing theological views, some of which may be radical and some conservative. This is the *de facto* position in most denominations today; all that remains is for us to cease to believe those who speak as though their view was the only tolerable one for Christians to adopt.

The next problem to arise for someone who agrees with the argument this far is obvious: What are you going to do when disagreement arises? It is all very well to urge Christians to accept the likelihood that views will differ. But does that mean that *any* view is tolerable within Christianity? Is there no way either of solving disputes about the faith between those who call themselves Christians, or of being able to present a working definition of what is involved in being a Christian? These kind of questions about the essential character of Christianity are important for two sorts of people. In the first place all Christian preachers and those who witness to their faith naturally want to be able to speak of 'the Christian faith' or 'The gospel' and to mean by it something clear and definite. It would be hopeless to hum and ha over possible viewpoints and opinions, or to become involved in complexities. The needs of evangelism require simplicity and directness about the content of the term 'Christian'. In this chapter, indeed in this book, it is not this need which we are seeking to meet; and it must be made clear from the start that, while I acknowledge that such a need exists, I am concerned with another reason for anxiety about the distinctive character of Christianity. This second need is felt acutely by theologians involved in discussions and disagreements about doctrine. To the layman the difficulties of theologians often appear to be largely of their own creation, and frequently enough while theologians disagree Church people simply get on with the job of living the Christian life together. This book is, however, designed to introduce the work of theologians and consequently the problem of disagreement must be squarely faced. The aim of the present chapter is to inquire whether theologians can refer to any kind of norm to help them when disagreement breaks out. And it is hoped that by showing the great complexity of this subject that a certain sympathy for their task may be generated!

A commonsense view of this question of the essential character of Christianity might well try to break in at this point. Obviously Christianity must consist in something; quite apart from what Christians might themselves need, ordinary linguistic usage demands some definition of the content of Christianity. It would be intolerable if the term 'Christian' could cover any view whatsoever. Even if Christianity were no more than an ideological tradition like Marxism, there would have to be views which one could identify as incompatible with or contradictory to its position. Linguistic use requires us to be able to justify the employment of terms like Christian, Marxist and Atheist by pointing to certain conventionally agreed notions in their context. It would be impossible to tolerate literally any view within Christianity.

If that is the case, then what are the 'conventionally agreed notions' by which the content of Christianity is defined, and what value are they in the event of dispute? The importance of these questions can be illustrated by a recent example. In the 1960s, partly as a result of some of the writings of Dietrich Bonhoeffer (1906–45), a school of 'theology' grew up in the United States which became known by the slogan, 'Death of God'. Its perfectly serious contention was that 'God' was no longer actual for man, and that 'theology' had to abandon both the term and the concept. When some more traditional theologians objected that this was no longer Christian theology but a form of Atheism, the question was rightly raised whether a theology in which the Devil had in effect perished had also any right to call itself Christian. For if it were true that Christ believed in the existence of God, it was also true that he believed in the existence of the Devil. Very clearly the content of Christianity could only be determined by reference to what Christ himself believed if one were prepared to accept all the consequences. If that were accepted as the criterion a very great deal of modern theology might turn out to be not Christian at all.

This dispute raised in an acute form the problem of the use of 'conventionally agreed notions' of the content of Christianity. If one were to ask the man in the street whether belief in God were part of being a Christian, doubtless the reply would be an emphatic affirmative. On such a basis belief in God is unquestionably a 'conventionally agreed notion' of the content of Christianity. But if the theologian says to the man in the street, 'You are wrong about this; God (as you conceive him) doesn't exist at all and is a disposable part of Christianity for the following reasons, (a), (b) and (c)', by reference to what are (a), (b) and (c) to be discussed? The commonsense position turns out on inspection to be of very little assistance when genuine fundamental dispute breaks out.

What then are the alternative norms by which such disputes might be settled? I have already indicated that the liberal theologian does not have available to him the final courts of appeal which have been used over the centuries, usually either the Bible or the solemn definitions of 'the Church'. If either of these could still be quoted as norms in the sense that the rules of chess are norms for the game of chess, then that which contradicted them could simply be ruled out of court. But unquestionably authoritative though the Bible and 'the Church' are in matters of Christian teaching, the position of the liberal theologian is that they do not and cannot function as that sort of norm. Are there any other alternatives?

One possibility, which has already been referred to above, is that true Christianity consists quite simply in the teaching of Christ. This is another popular, commonsense position of some attractiveness. For it offers the hope of being able to cut away much of what is said to be the obtrusive paraphernalia of the theology of the Church and even of the apostle Paul. Sometimes also a critic will attempt to attribute some of the 'difficult' sayings put into the mouth of Jesus to the beliefs of the later Church. But whether or not this procedure is adopted, it is precisely the presence of 'difficult' sayings in the gospels which makes the whole attempt to define Christianity solely by reference to the teaching of Jesus such a doubtful enterprise. For we only know the teaching of Jesus at second hand, as it was reported in documents written down some little time later. And unless the teaching of Jesus itself requires us to believe that the documents in which his teaching is reported are all without error (which would in any case be a circular position), we are bound to be uncertain in the end whether and to what extent distortion of his teaching may have crept in. Thus we would be unable to use the documents themselves with complete confidence, and our account of the original teaching would be to a greater or lesser extent conjectural.

But there would be a further problem to face. Precisely because some of the sayings attributed to Jesus appear to us to be 'difficult', it is necessary to ask whether in any case Christianity consists in believing what Jesus believed and taught. Notorious problems in this area in the last hundred years have been demonology and the (so-called) second coming of Christ. As belief in the existence and activity of demons declined from the eighteenth century, the question of whether Jesus believed in their existence and activity has been raised, and of whether, if he did so believe, that belief necessarily implies that his followers must believe likewise. Similarly, it appears from the New Testament that many early Christians expected an immediate return of Christ, and some reconstructions of Jesus' teaching in the last seventy years attribute this expectation to Jesus' own hopes. In both cases one is faced with the question of whether Christian belief in the divinity of Christ is compatible with recognition that Jesus might have held and taught (what might be said to be) factually incorrect beliefs.

These questions, precisely because they are to some extent matters of historical judgement, are exceedingly difficult to decide and cannot be fully discussed here. Even if it were reasonably certain that Jesus believed in the existence and activity of demons, it would still be a considerable problem for interpretation whether he taught such a belief as a constructive truth of his teaching. It would be a further problem what relation such a teaching would have to the widespread modern supposition that demons do not exist. We would immediately become involved in a discussion of the senses in which a belief may or may not be true. Is it, for example, as true to say of a man that he is possessed of a demon as to say that he is a neurotic hysteric; or is it a truth of a different kind; or is it quite simply untrue? The discussion of this would introduce considerations which would considerably complicate the apparently simple appeal to the teaching of Jesus as the decisive

D

norm in questions about the content of Christianity. Once again, although it cannot be doubted that the religion which takes its name from Jesus of Nazareth must rely upon the authority of his teaching, the appeal to it cannot be as straight-forwardly conclusive as one might have been wished. Are there yet other possibilities?

It is at this point that we are bound to admit that no very satisfactory alternatives have yet been produced. Christian theology has, in effect, only faced the problem of trying to provide a new way of arriving at the essential content of Christianity in the last 200 years. With some notable exceptions the issue has been frequently enough avoided. For most practical purposes the Western public has retained a 'con-ventionally agreed notion' of the content of Christianity to which theologians have been able to appeal. Popular books on the Christian faith have appeared in great numbers laying out the 'essentials', or 'restating' them for 'modern man', without very much investigation of why certain doctrines of the traditional Christian faith should have been included and others omitted. A diligent reading of such books inevitably reveals that what one author omits another retains, and vice versa. One frequently finds that in order to establish or rein-force the persuasiveness of one particular doctrine in Christian theology the author confidently quotes this or that traditional authority, and yet is strangely silent when another passage in the same authority counts against his argument in another place. Beneath the smooth surface of a persuasive sounding 'restatement' lie assumptions which are too infrequently exposed and examined.

Is it the case then that there are *no* ways of resolving arguments about the content of Christianity? We have already stated that pluriformity of belief is to be expected in Christianity. Must we conclude, in the absence of any agreed alternative, that anyone's belief has as much right to be called Christian as anyone else's; that although the term 'Christian' derives its meaning for the practical purposes of discourse from the 'conventionally agreed notions' of Christianity at any one time, theology cannot provide guidelines, norms or authorities by which disputes in matters of doctrine might be settled? Defenders of this view, which is coming to be of some importance in modern theological thinking, sometimes add that though there are no formal, written guidelines, it is precisely the work of the Holy Spirit in the individual and the whole Church to lead Christians into all truth; and that, although confusion and uncertainty reign in matters of doctrine and theory, in practice and particularly in worship Christians are being led and arguments are being resolved by the hidden guidance of the Holy Spirit.

The difficulty with this position is that it does not escape from the confusion and uncertainty it proposes to accept. For the view that the Holy Spirit guides the Church is itself a doctrine based on scripture and the teaching of the Church; and as a doctrine it, too, does not escape from the challenge to its authority which might be mounted on the basis of actual experience. For as we look at Church history, it might be asked, what real reason have we to believe that the Holy Spirit guides the Church? One very experienced German Protestant theologian wrote in the nineteenth century, long before all the abominations committed with the sanction of religion in the twentieth,

> it is only a really strong faith in the invisible that, amid the miry abominations and miserable trivialities of Church history, can trace the advancing power of Christ over this world at all.*

Are we really supposed to believe that the Church comes in the end to the right decision in all matters of dispute, and, if so,

---

* A. Ritschl, *The Christian Doctrine of Justification and Reconciliation* (Edinburgh, 1902), III, p. 460.

over how long a period? Moreover there is real danger of coming to believe that whatever is, is right; that is, of depriving a protesting minority of its right to continue opposition to a view which a majority has come to accept. The view that error has no rights has been one of the justifications of persecution offered by totalitarian regimes, both ecclesiastical and secular, for many centuries.

Such pernicious consequences naturally enough are not envisaged in any modern form of a doctrine of divine guidance; but they nevertheless remain, as two recent examples show. In both of these the disputes concerned ecumenical discussion, where personal, national and party considerations all too readily become involved in the theological points being debated. In one case concerning conversations between Presbyterians and Anglicans, a minority party suddenly discovered that a certain course of action recommended by the majority was apparently being claimed to have the backing of the Holy Spirit. From the premise that reunion of Churches was part of the divine will, an illegal deduction had been made that a particular reunion proposal was revelation of divine guidance.* A second, similar instance concerned the Anglican–Methodist reunion proposals, where similar claims were made for a still more clearly politically contrived solution to a disagreement about the ministry of the Church. The danger of the spiritual blackmail of a minority is obviously not to be discounted when claims are made for divine guidance in relation to disputed matters. Such claims have to be made with caution; indeed it is surely open to dispute whether the doctrine of the Holy Spirit ought ever be used in this immediate way in relation to the human administration of Churches.

The problem, then, remains with us and awaits some answer. How may Christianity be defined? The first thing is to note

* See the justified, if over-rhetorical protest, in I. Henderson, *Power without Glory: a Study in Ecumenical Politics* ((London, 1967).

that a definition may serve two purposes, (a) descriptive and (b) normative. Our ultimate aim is to discover a definition which will function as some kind of norm in the situation of doctrinal disagreement between Christians. But we may begin our answer to the question, How may Christianity be defined, by looking at some of the complexities of a purely descriptive account of its content.

In the first place a descriptive definition could never be a final definition, since Christianity is an historical phenomenon. In this respect a definition of Christianity would be like character definition. There could be a multiplicity of character portraits, but none would be final, since new events might disclose further latent traits. Nor would any character definition of the past accurately describe what might be apparent at the present. Character definition is parallel in another respect, also, in as much as it allows for a multiplicity of points of view, all of which may be helpful in building up an overall picture. And it may be readily accepted that a complex phenomenon like the Christian religion does need to be viewed from many differing points of view before its essential character can be grasped.

But even if one were able with great difficulty to assemble a set of accounts of the essential character of Christianity as an historical phenomenon which did justice to its complexity and inner variety, what precise use would this description be in helping to create a *normative* definition? Or to put it in another way, even if one could describe what Christianity *was*, how would it help us solve the problem of what it *ought to be*?

The answer lies in the special relationship which Christianity has with history. A comparison between Christianity and an ideology like humanism will help to make the point. Ideologies, or idea systems, exist as a set of views about the world whose content may be explained and examined quite independently of the history of how they came to exist. It is not specially relevant to whether such ideas are true that Mr X and Dr Y professed to believe them at such and such a time in history.

Not so with Christianity. This only exists because of the event of Jesus at a specific time in history. Because Christianity is *about* Jesus, about his birth, death and resurrection, its character is fundamentally shaped by the fact that Jesus actually existed. It is true that ideological interpretations of Christianity have been offered since the Enlightenment, in which the idea content of Christian teaching is separated from the history of the event of Jesus.* But these interpretations have never had much popularity, a fact which is an instructive instance of continuity of substance in the development of Christian doctrine. Christian belief in the event of Christ and in Christ's continued presence in the historical process makes discovery of what happened in the past a very important part of the constructive task of Christian theology. Thus one of the inescapable tasks of theology is to keep the past history of the Christian Church, including the New Testament period, vividly fresh in the imagination of the present Church. The essential character of Christianity can only be investigated in a normative way, when the descriptive task has been as honestly and thoroughly done as possible.

The descriptive task of investigating the essence of Christianity in its twenty centuries of history is, obviously enough, a vast one. For what has to be studied is not merely the history of the large 'central' Churches, but all the debates and variety of views to which the event of Christ has given rise. Indeed a good deal hangs upon the student's preparedness to consider all aspects, since it is unquestionably a characteristic of Chris-

* E.g. in D. F. Strauss's *Life of Jesus* (4th ed., 1840; E.T. by George Eliot, 1848), where the author, having expounded his view that the gospels are largely mythical, interprets the life of Jesus to mean that 'humanity' dies, rises and ascends to heaven, by constantly negating its attachment to the baser side of life and uniting itself to higher, spiritual values. See § 151.

tianity that it is capable of the great variety of interpretation which it has in fact received. To impose one's own standards of normality upon one's selection of material to study is radically to diminish the chances that such study will yield the width of perspective upon the character of Christianity that is to be hoped for.

When this study has been undertaken carefully and thoroughly rather surprising facts begin to emerge. An excellent example of one such study and the kind of results to which it leads is a book by an American theologian, H. Richard Niebuhr, *Christ and Culture*.* This reviews the history of how the relationship between Christianity and civilization has been viewed by Christian theologians over the centuries, and shows how great a variety of attitudes have been held. Niebuhr classifies these attributes into types and shows how they have persisted from earliest times. Although the book is primarily an historical study he himself appears to prefer one of the five types of interpretation.

But the mere fact of the variety itself calls for some explanation. How can Christianity, on a matter so basic as the Christian's attitude towards civilisation, speak with so many conflicting opinions? The inevitable answer is, I believe, that Christianity far from being a single religious group, is a family of religions with a common focus. The complexity of describing the character of Christianity is not merely like that of describing the character of a single individual, but rather more like the task of discerning and describing family likeness in a large group of related individuals of different ages and stages of maturity.

It is at this point that the descriptive task must give way to normative. For there comes a time when awareness of the complexity of the beliefs, practices and attitudes of those who have called themselves Christians over the centuries simply

* First published 1951, Harper Torchbook edition (New York, 1956).

cries out for some kind of critical, normative evaluation. We may allow in our descriptive work that all those who claim the title Christian should be so regarded if they can show that they have drawn on elements of traditional Christianity. But the sheer variety of such elements requires a second, normative use of the term Christian. Otherwise the quest for the essential character of Christianity would transform itself into the quest for some common denominator between groups, which could only be an element of the utmost triviality.

Thus for the normative quest it is not a matter of identifying what, if anything, may be common to all who profess the name of Christian. It is the more difficult and adventurous task of trying to state what *ought* to characterise *true* Christianity; a definition, in other words, that would be of some use in doctrinal disagreements. Strange to say, we have some such notion even in character definition when we consider how a person *ought* to act if he were to be *true to himself*; that is to say, a self-consistent course of behaviour.

What then would a normative definition of Christianity be like? We may attempt to list its characteristics. First, it must be a definition which takes into account the facts, mentioned above, of the variety of forms which Christianity has assumed in history. Secondly, it must be demonstrably a self-consistent definition (that is, true to itself, as suggested above), which highlights aspects of what has continuously appeared as part of the content of Christianity from the first. In practice it will be able to achieve this characteristic by being consistently based on exegesis of the New Testament. Thirdly, a normative definition of Christianity must itself be true. It would not be possible, for example, for part of this definition to be at once self-consistent and false. If Christianity claims to be true, though there are admittedly many senses of the term 'true', then a normative definition of Christian faith cannot be allowed to contain untruth.

I believe that it is possible to offer a normative definition of Christianity which embodies these characteristics and which can operate as some kind of norm in the presence of doctrinal disagreements. This definition, which I entitle 'the character or spirit of Christ' and which is expounded more fully in Chapter 7, is not a simple, normative statement. It is a highly complex notion because, as the study of the historically deployed character of Christianity shows, the Christian faith is itself highly complex. It expresses, for a start, a bewildering interplay of doctrinal, ethical and devotional elements. It is, furthermore, the attempted reduplication of the many-sided event of Jesus himself through the medium of the individual lives of his disciples.

A definition which aims to do some justice to this complexity is likely of course, to be difficult to use in practice. And this is its chief disadvantage. However, we have to remind ourselves in the twentieth century that, despite the long history of Christianity, the attempt to find some normative definition of Christianity to replace the older straightforwardly authoritative courts of appeal is only two centuries old at the most. Compared with earlier times the present situation may appear to some as chaotic as a state of total normlessness. The constant temptation for Christians, and for theologians no less than for others, will be simplification and over-emphasis, the reduction of the complex task of preserving the character of Christ in Christian thought and witness, to a few striking maxims.

All this is not to deny the function of striking maxims and simplifications in other contexts, for example in preaching. It is certainly not being claimed here that the Christian life can only be lived or believed in by those conscious of the complexities of doctrinal discussion. Simplification has an important function in morality and in religious belief. In both these cases practical considerations rightly loom large, and it may with full justice be claimed that for all practical purposes certain clear guidelines are essential. The ten commandments, the Lord's prayer and the creeds of the Church are precisely that.

Here, however, we are not so concerned with the practical, as with the theoretical. Discussion of disagreements in Christian theology is not the same thing as preaching or witnessing to the Christian faith. The use of simplification in the latter is in many respects valid, where in the former it would be stultifying.

So the aim of this chapter has been the limited one of illustrating the complexity of being a Christian theologian in the twentieth century arguing out the problem of doctrinal disagreements and how they may be resolved. It is, further, the hope of the writer that a certain sympathy for the difficulty of the task may have been aroused!

4
OBJECTIONS TO CHRISTIANITY

IT should obviously be asked whether any of this interest in the internal disputes of theology has any basis at all; and it should also be realised how modern a question this in fact is. The reader who picks up a book about theology or religion is quite likely to be a religious person; but his neighbour or teen-age son is quite as likely to be an atheist. For centuries theologians and religious people have been used to disputes about religion of a primarily internal character, whether this or that aspect of their belief should be interpreted in this or that way. But now these disputes have been and are being overtaken in urgency by the radical, outside question whether or not there is any basis at all for worrying further about questions of religious belief. And the freedom to ask such a question has only recently been acquired. The more a religion appears to be dominant in a society, be that society Arab, European, Asian or Jewish, the more daring a thing it appears to declare oneself a total non-believer. In Europe and North America today, following the widespread growth of publicly expressed agnostic and atheist opinions this has become no longer a remarkable position. And consequently there has taken place a shift of interest in theological and religious affairs to the radical, external question of the truth of any religious position at all. It is precisely because of this shift of interest that theology, as it has been understood and practised in these countries until comparatively recently, has the appearance of 'irrelevance'. It

57

seems to deal, that is, with questions which are no longer of urgent importance. There is no use, it would seem, discussing how to balance apparently contradictory aspects of the nature of God (for example, his love and his justice), if there is no reason to believe that he exists at all.

The considerations urged against belief in God are sometimes of an entirely general nature. That is to say if they are true they invalidate any conception of God whatever. The most usual arguments here are developed by way of the social and psychological function of religion. The critic looks at the phenomenon of religion with the question, What caused it to spring into being? If he can show the phenomenon to be sufficiently explained by its social or psychological function, then he may conclude that it is not necessary to invoke any supernatural causes for its existence. It is true, of course, that many sociologists and psychologists do not feel that it is any part of their discipline to comment upon the truth or otherwise of the claims made by any particular religion. But defenders both of religion and of agnosticism or atheism are not slow to point to the personal beliefs of leading sociologists and psychologists. Emile Durkheim (1858–1917), one of the great makers of modern sociological theory and a writer on religion,* though of Jewish parentage, was an agnostic. Sigmund Freud (1856–1939) also a Jew by birth, notoriously urged that religion was a neurosis.

Whether or not the scholars themselves take up a position in regard to the truth of the claims of the religion they study by sociological or psychological methods, it remains in principle an askable question whether their findings do not constitute a sufficient explanation of the origin of religion. Explanations, of course, are of various types. It is comparatively simple to explain the workings of a motor car because one can use a total

* *The Elementary Forms of the Religious Life* (in French 1912; E.T. London, 1954).

mechanical diagram. Explanations of human behaviour are much more difficult, however, because despite all the research, no one has yet produced such a diagram to help us. A 1930 Rolls Royce works in the way the engineers of that date designed it. But the human beings born in 1930 to different parents in every corner of the globe are infinitely more various. Explanations of the behaviour of these beings do not begin to lend themselves to the type of exactitude possible in the case of the motor car. Even if we are certain that a mechanical diagram is the kind we require, we must also be aware how far short we fall at present from being able to provide one.

In areas where we would desperately like to have an explanation, and where there seems no possible way of getting one, human beings frequently and characteristically grasp at straws. Of nothing is this more true than of human, especially odd human behaviour. In this area 'explanations' often serve an important psychological function in reassuring us of the normality and orderliness, according to our current conceptions of normality and order, of our existence. When we contemplate religious behaviour we may easily fall into this danger. For here especially we may be at the mercy of our own predilections. The odder the activity is felt to be, the greater the desire to be satisfied with a social or psychological explanation. This may be true for the modern Christian looking at primitive or ancient religious rites, or the modern agnostic or atheist looking at contemporary Christianity. In either case the behaviour he is examining may appear to threaten his own understanding of life and he may feel satisfied with a wholly insufficient explanation. Such explanations are really 'analgesic pills which dull the aches of incomprehension without going to their causes'.*

But this is not the only difficulty about the argument from

* This splendid phrase is P. B. Medawar's in *The Art of the Soluble*, (London, 1967), p. 87, though used here in a different context.

the social and psychological function of religion. Still more serious is the difficulty of identifying and isolating 'religion' in order to study it. What is religion? In popular western usage 'religion' may mean a very dilute form of basic Christian belief and practice. Thus 'religious education' is very frequently conceived in this country to be basic Christian morality. But it is very easy to show that this morality is not 'necessarily' or 'distinctively' religious at all, in the sense that it can be and is practised by people without religious convictions.

When one does try to state definitively what religion is, one is faced with a simply stupendous intellectual task. One has to gather together all the forms of religion which are known to have been practised by man, together with the various theories of its origins offered by sociologists, anthropologists and psychologists, and try to reach some conclusion concerning its essence. The difficulty is that one has to start with definition in order to make any progress in the study at all. Is my visiting of my infirm grandmother with a bunch of flowers and three library books an example of religious behaviour? Is my attending a beautifully sung Anglican Evensong an example of religious behaviour? The answer depends upon one's definition of religion. It also depends upon whether these activities count as activities characteristic of the religion which I profess. In the context of some religions certain aesthetic or moral activities do not in any way follow from the content of the religion. We are left with an extremely perplexing conclusion, namely that the definition of religion with which one works may be quite insufficient *even to identify* some behaviour as religious behaviour in the context of its own system.

In practice the psychological or sociological observer may be forced to say at the beginning of his work, 'for the purposes of this discussion, I am regarding such and such as religious behaviour'. But even if this is permissible a further difficulty then arises whether in isolating certain types or instances of behaviour as religious he has not interfered from the beginning with the very phenomenon he hoped to study. This same difficulty exists in many scientific fields, in which careful observation can only be undertaken when the observer has interfered with the environment of his chosen subject. The conclusion is not that his study is valueless, but that allowance must be made for the effect of the interference. And in the case of the observing of religious behaviour from a psychological or sociological point of view the degree of interference may again vary markedly from religion to religion in accordance with its own distinctive internal structure.

The conclusion of this discussion must be that the general objection to religion, as a phenomenon which may be explained sufficiently by psychological or sociological studies, is not a particularly well-founded one. An alternative attack is sometimes developed by way of biological science. This attack assumes that religion is concerned with a non-material being or beings whose acts or influences may be detected in human life at a spiritual, or at any rate a non-physical level. Biological science, it is asserted, knows nothing of these alleged influences; quite the contrary, it increasingly reveals that the phenomenon of life may be explained in purely mechanical terms.

I believe it is possible to be quite brief with this attack. For on the one hand many scientists themselves dispute the claim that man is nothing but a complex machine;* on the other hand it is far from clear on logical grounds that even a fully determinist account of the mechanism of the brain would exclude all freedom of will.† The most that could be claimed for a scientific argument against any and all religion is that it is a theory projected out of one department of enquiry to cover

* See the interesting collection of essays edited by Arthur Koestler and J. R. Smythies *Beyond Reductionism* (London, 1969).
† See the arguments of D. M. MacKay in *Freedom of Action in a Mechanistic Universe* (Cambridge, 1967).

all possible departments of inquiry. That the theory operates in its own area cannot be disputed. It is one way of seeing man which has made possible great advances in, for example, medicine. But to claim the prestige of scientific research for the speculative projection of the theory is quite untenable. As a speculation it remains nothing more than a possibility which has to be investigated along with other possibilities. It could not be claimed that anything like proof could be adduced for it.

If the general objections to religion are seen to be somewhat lacking in coherence and conclusive force, by contrast it would seem that the attacks on a particular religion are far more effective. As we have observed, most people in the Western world, when they speak of religion, have in mind Judaism and Christianity; so also most people, when they speak of God, have in mind God as he is spoken of in the context of these two faiths. Objections to these two faiths, if valid, do not dispose of all religious belief; nor, conversely, do objections to other religions (primitive religions, for example) dispose of these. This fact ought to be borne in mind in observing that as a matter of history most of the arguments of modern atheism have been developed in the context of Christian civilization.

The remainder of this chapter is devoted therefore to an examination of the *specific* objections to belief in God as he is conceived of within Christianity. Three objections may be made in particular. The first is of primarily psychological force. Is it conceivable, it is said, with our present astronomical knowledge of the immensity of the universe, that the alleged creator of it would be concerned with man's detailed behaviour in the way he is said to be by the Jewish and the Christian religions? And is it conceivable that Jesus Christ should have the cosmic significance he is supposed to have? The sheer size of the cosmos, its age and probable future makes the doings in Jerusalem two thousand years ago seem incredibly parochial and insignificant. The second argument appeals to logic. The

Christian faith is a whole nest of contradictions, disguised as paradoxes. It satisfies few if any of the criteria for meaningful discourse and relies upon confusion to preserve an appearance of deep and rich significance. And the third argument is based on moral judgement. The Christian religion has in practice issued in some extremely undesirable consequences, among them superstition, intolerance, suppression of free inquiry, repression of natural instinct, and resignation in the face of injustice or adversity.*

The objections briefly mentioned here are very substantial; they cannot be dismissed cursorily, and they have called forth a considerable literature. The traditional answering discipline is known as apologetics, and this has been practised in Britain since the eighteenth century with great energy. The kind of book which is written in order to meet these objections may be seen, for example, in John Hick's *Evil and the God of Love*.† The opening words of this book state that 'the fact of evil constitutes the most serious objection there is to the Christian belief in a God of love',‡ and the author goes on to show a possible way in which that belief and the facts of evil do not collide with each other. Books on Christianity and science have been published in large numbers both by theologians and scientists, which have attempted various means of avoiding or reconciling apparent conflict in these areas.§ Other works on Christian ethics attempt, by means of explanation and the working out of particular examples, to avoid the moral critique of Christianity.¶

---

* See further *Objections to Christian Belief*, ed. A. R. Vidler (London, 1963), essays by four Christian theologians.
 † London, 1966.   ‡ *Ibid.*, p. xi.
 § See, for example, I. G. Barbour, *Issues in Science and Religion* (London, 1967).
 ¶ See, for example, H. Rashdall, *Conscience and Christ* (London, 1916), ch. IV. There is comparatively little recent apologetic writing in Christian ethics.

E

No attempt can be made here to present the various replies which have been made. The summaries of such arguments are necessarily superficial, and we have to beware of a less than honest investment in the outcome of the discussion, on either side of the apologetic fence. The prejudicing of a discussion by the use of pejorative terms—my presentation of the arguments against Christianity contained a large number of these—or the commendation of an agreeable opinion by an emotionally loaded adjective are the (often unconscious) devices of a partisan frame of mind. It is the case that, even when properly spelt out, the charges against Christianity are serious; and they merit the quality of attention which is given them by the larger works which have been cited.

At the same time we may profitably look at one exceedingly curious aspect of the situation. The objections lodged against Christianity treat it as a belief system, allegedly dependent upon divine revelation for its existence. The objections conclude that because these beliefs are incorrect or incoherent they cannot possibly be based upon such divine revelation. The critic takes the beliefs and sets them in contradistinction to what he considers to be the facts of the matter. His procedure is quite plain because he is operating from *outside* the belief system; he considers himself to be in the position, that is, of an impartial judge weighing evidence from two witnesses, and of finding one to be a spinner of fairy-tales. Now there are two courses open to the Christian believer who wants to reply. The first is to accept the critic's construction of the position, and to seek to show from the witness-box, so to speak, that no such contradictions exist between him and the evidence of the facts. On the other hand he may utterly and completely deny the critic's construction of the scene and turn the tables by putting *himself* in the seat of judgement and judging the critic by what *he* considers to be the facts. The tradition of apologetics has very largely been to accept the former alternative and to attempt a reply to objections from a standpoint which the objector would recognise as valid; that is to say, one which would not, in the objector's eyes, beg the question.

The problem is, of course, that the believer's belief *does* beg the question. And the believer's point of view in the dispute can only be properly represented if he is prepared to state unequivocally how he himself sees the matter. It is one of the most important lessons which the very great Swiss theologian, Karl Barth (1886–1968), taught modern theology, that apologetics cannot by its very nature represent the Christian point of view, because it is conditioned, not to say distorted, by being argued from the standpoint of the objector. One element of the Christian view of a dispute about the validity of his faith is that the objector is not in a position in which he might appreciate the strength of the Christian's case for believing, and that nothing short of belief could put him into such a position. That is to say the Christian doubts whether, in such a matter, the neutrality of an impartial judge is attainable. The choice is not between belief, impartiality and disbelief, but between belief and disbelief.

The essential point being made here is that *the content of what the Christian believer believes is in certain vital respects unlike anything else which might be a matter of belief in religion, science, ethics or aesthetics.* That is to say, by reason of faithfulness to the content of what he believes, he is unable to offer exact parallels or comparisons. For belief in God, as he is understood in Christian faith, is strictly not like any other belief, there being no one comparable with him. And belief in Jesus Christ is also in certain respects unparalleled and incomparable. By reference to what, other than God himself and Christ himself, can one establish the validity for believing in them? But if one *does* appeal to them, then is not one begging the whole question?

The difficulty is absolutely crucial to the consideration of objections to Christian belief. Though the Christian may for the sake of argument, or out of courtesy, temporarily try to see things from the objector's point of view, what he may do by such a procedure is strictly limited. He may, for example, be able to point out internal inconsistencies in the objector's presentation of his case; he may also be able to point out discrepancies between the type of arguments he brings against Christian belief and the type of arguments he uses to support his own belief. But if he wishes to validate his own convictions, he will need very carefully to consider what kind of arguments, based on what kind of assumptions, he will be able to offer.

We may take an example from the problem of evil, *Si deus bonus, unde malum*; if God is good, whence comes evil? The theist may try with varying degrees of success to show that most or many forms of evil are conducive to greater goods, or are the natural corollary of an environment in which greater goods are possible. But if that theist is a Christian, and he believes that 'God loved the world so much that he gave his only Son' (John 3.16), this makes a very important difference to his whole view of evil. Nor can he bring in that belief in an appendix, since, if he believes it, it radically conditions his whole understanding of God. And if he is not to mislead opponents who take a different view of the significance of evil, he had better state at the earliest possible moment how he understands the facts to be. For the Christian believer the significance of Christ is determinative for his attitude towards any fact of existential moment. In the case of evil this means that he sees evil as something upon which the judgement of God has been passed in Christ. He is unable to agree with a non-believer on a neutral description of 'the facts' of evil.

What is more, because in the context of his faith what he believes about God's act in Jesus Christ is in important respects unpredictable and unprecedented, he will not be able to offer *apart from the belief itself* any hope of finding valid grounds for believing it. God's judgement upon evil in Christ is not an instance of God's activity which might have been inferred from the significance of evil considered apart from that judgement. Thus the validity of believing that God *has* so acted in Christ and that the significance of evil *is* such as it appears in the light of that activity can only be assessed by considering the belief itself. This is only one example. But it establishes the general point made earlier that only by reference to God himself and to Christ himself can one hope to establish the validity of believing in them.

At this point, of course, the non-believer is apt to become annoyed and the believer himself somewhat nervous. What the Christian appears to be saying in effect is, 'Take it or leave it; see things my way or not at all'. And such statements seem at once arrogant and foolish; arrogant, because they imply that only Christians are right, and foolish, because such an assumption instantly antagonises one's companions in discussion.

Before admitting that there are indeed matters which can be profitably discussed by believers and non-believers, *proper recognition must be given to the bold claims and searching requirements of the Christian position.* In the first place, two hundred years of trimming the Christian gospel to contemporary opinion has shown how dangerous it is for the Christian to be uncritically prepared to accept whatever the non-believer may assert to be the ultimate court of appeal. We should by now have learnt to beware of the unexamined assumptions in what may at any time pass as self-evident truth, both in philosophy and science. If the Christian has any convictions that he has a source of truth available to him which may not be available to a scientist or philosopher working independently, he may need to develop a certain obstinacy in relation to the arguments used to support alternative views. The theological task is not complete when every latest opinion has been assimilated into the structure of Christian belief. The theologian's task is *critical* at every step.

And in the second place, even if the Christian considers the whole question of the 'image' of his faith (as a Public Relations Officer might consider the 'image' of a political party) it is very far from clear that the posture of the pragmatist is that which most widely appeals. The energetic independence of mind which characterised the young Church, and which is written on every page of the New Testament, is built inextricably into the fabric of the Christian faith itself. It is true that Paul and the writer to the Hebrews used argument (though of a rather specialised variety) and it may also be true that we can see nothing impatiently arrogant about Jesus' method of preaching; but both Paul and Jesus struck people in many different ways. Undoubtedly the independent, prophetic authority of the voice of the young Church struck (and still strikes) the orthodox Jew as unwarranted and objectionable self-assertiveness. But then, as now, the Church had to ask itself with whom and for what reason it wished to be popular. And those who read the history of the Christians in Nazi Germany must realise that nothing is so necessary as a long, cool look at all talk of 'popularity' and 'image', and that a long-term view must be taken of the significance of the public reputation of the Church at any given moment.

The 'take it or leave it' stance has, therefore, genuinely valuable elements within it. At the same time it must be said that *there are obviously areas of common ground which can be discussed by believer and non-believer with considerable profit*, at least from the Christian's point of view. The Christian's position is not that his own view is infallibly correct in every detail. But his position is that he has a view-point which he can defend as true, which puts him in a specially privileged position in discussion of matters of existential moment. The special privilege consists entirely in the significance for him of the person of Jesus Christ. But it is perfectly possible, and indeed profitable, that this significance should be the subject of discussion between believer and non-believer.

Let us enumerate clearly the topics which may be discussed. First there is the historicity of Jesus. As a matter of fact he lived at a certain time, died, and (so most Christians have believed) rose from death. As a matter of fact he taught certain things and made a certain impression. Whatever may be claimed, with varying degrees of justifiability, as historically verifiable, forms an extremely important element of publicly available information, and thus common ground, between believer and non-believer. How much common ground exists in this way has been much discussed and is the subject of wide disagreements. But that discussion too is a public one, and is very important and valuable.

Secondly, there are the lives of Christians. These too are public property, being both actual and observable and therefore properly an area of common ground. It is asserted by Christians that these lives are of evidential value in considering the significance of Christ for our own day; it may indeed be said that they form some part of the evidence for the resurrection of Christ. Discussion of them is therefore fully possible and valuable.

Thirdly, the Christian faith, consequent upon Jesus' ministry, has a certain shape and content. In its totality it is said not merely to be true, or to contain individual true statements, but to be *the truth*; to have, that is, a certain wholeness or universality about it. This quality has in various ages been variously identified. One particularly influential strand of thought has been so-called Logos theology. Christ is said in John 1 to be the 'Logos', and some early Greek theologians explored the idea that 'Logos' meant the principle of rationality underlying all existence. Certainly the view that rationality is the prime characteristic of *human* existence is dominant today, though the precise interpretation of what constitutes rational discourse and behaviour varies widely. The Christian may or may not use the term 'rationality' to describe what he wishes to say about 'the truth', in the sense of the wholeness and universality of the Christian faith. But whatever precise word he uses, the concept will necessarily include human experience and inevitably incorporate an appeal to that experience. To put it another way, the wholeness of the Christian faith involves it in interpreting the whole of existence. Christian theology can therefore never be merely a description of the internal rationale of the private experience of Christian believers. The world and human kind existed before Christ, and much of it still exists in ignorance or defiance of him. For the Christian faith to be whole and universal, this experience also must be incorporated. It is thus clear that interpretation of the whole human situation forms an area of common ground between believers and non-believers.

These are the three main areas where there is common ground between believer and non-believer, and which can form the agreed basis of any discussion. If the claims which the Christian makes about his faith are wrong, they will be wrong in these areas. In these areas he is vulnerable to attack; and, conversely, in these areas lie the considerable strengths of his position. If he wishes to establish to a non-believer the validity of his faith, his arguments are the most effective when they are based on these areas of common ground. He may, also, as was mentioned above, counterattack by exposing the inadequacies of the alternative views of his partner in discussion.

Thus a rather complex pattern begins to emerge of the kind of arguments which establish the validity of believing the Christian faith to be true. First of all, it is a pattern which is distinctive of and appropriate to the particular content of the Christian faith, and may not be characteristic of any other faith at all. Believing the Christian faith to be true need not be like believing any other faith or any other belief. Thus the validity of the Christian faith is not be to considered apart from the content of that faith and the claims for a specially privileged point of view made by that faith. Secondly, that faith quite characteristically makes bold claims for itself, and requires the believer to be searchingly critical of views, opinions and arguments developed independently of it. And, thirdly, again because of its special content, it provides areas of common ground—the story of Jesus, the lives of Christians and the whole area of human experience—in which its claims to be true can be properly discussed by believer and non-believer alike. When these are considered the factual basis of the Christian faith begins to emerge, and a discussion can develop in which the Christian is not required as a premise of the debate to lay on one side the very considerations which justify his holding the views he does.

5
JESUS AND THE WITNESS
TO JESUS

I consider in this second part of the book some of the material with which Christian theology deals and the considerations which are relevant to writing theology today. Naturally we must first deal with Jesus and the witness to Jesus, which are inseparably the foundations of the Christian faith. For the distinctiveness of the Christian faith depends upon that historical person and upon the effect he produced, leading men to write of him in the way they did. This chapter is mainly concerned with the implications of the fact that this distinctiveness is not that of a timelessly true set of ideas, but is a history both of an individual and of his effect on others.

We are bound to begin by some comments on the way in which the Bible, and particularly the New Testament, is popularly regarded. For nothing short of a revolution in attitude towards the New Testament will enable us to see the freshness and originality of the documents which comprise it. The New Testament is often treated with an awe which borders on the superstitious. From an early age children are fed on gospel stories, which, because they are about Christ, arc regarded by parents and teachers as immune from criticism. We are beginning to discover how deleterious are the effects of educating young children in essentially magical views of the supernatural element of the gospels. In this way we have created for many young people a formidable sense of unreality, which eventually acts as a barrier to comprehension whenever biblical narratives are rehearsed.

But this is not all. Again, particularly with regard to stories about Jesus, the Church has done itself a profound disservice by making inflated claims for the moral, aesthetic and spiritual excellence of Jesus. Using the doctrine of the divinity of Christ as a kind of justification, properties have been claimed for the stories about, and teaching of Jesus which the narrative itself only partially supports. Thus it is sometimes said that the poetic, parable-telling technique of Jesus was unsurpassed or that the stories show that his love for man was inexhaustible, or that he suffered unflinchingly the most painful death that man could devise. The commendatory adjectives, undoubtedly meant as a sincere tribute to the narratives, nevertheless cumulatively have a deadening effect; and on inspection many of them turn out to be baseless. The figure of the man Jesus dies the death of a thousand superlatives. It seems that both Jesus and the witness to Jesus have suffered grievously from the enthusiasm of Christians. At one time it was thought shocking for the Bible to be treated 'as any other book'. We may now be able to see with a certain clarity some of the possible *benefits* to be reaped from reading the New Testament books as one might read other ancient documents.

One must not, of course, omit to mention the chief reason for handling the Bible with reverence, which is the doctrine of the inspiration of the Scriptures by the Holy Spirit. Particularly for those who stand in the heritage of the Reformation and evangelical Christianity, this doctrine has effectively determined the position of unique reverence which the Bible occupies in the Christian faith. The story of the dismantling of this doctrine and its reconstruction in another form, as a result of the literary and historical investigation of the documents is probably too familiar to need retelling.* And there are still many Christians who are far from satisfied with the

* See S. Neill, *The Interpretation of the New Testament* (1861–1961), (Cambridge, 1964).

procedures or the results of this process. But even conservative scholars deplore the superstitious use of the Bible
and of the procedures of 'proof-texting' employed in earlier
centuries. The conviction that the Bible must be read and
studied in close relationship to its background has grown, and
there is wide agreement on the gains to be had from a more
sober consideration of the distinctiveness of early Christianity
in its contemporary setting.* For about one hundred years
now, Christians have had the advantage of an independent,
and often perceptive, treatment of the gospels by Jewish
writers. As a counterweight to the exaggeration and bias
exhibited in much Christian commentary, a reading of such
Jewish work is a salutary experience.†

Jesus was a Jew. It is not possible to grasp either the setting
of his teaching or the situation of the primitive Christian com-
munities unless we understand the Jewishness of Jesus. The
whole New Testament bears witness to the early Church's
struggle to define itself in relation to historic Judaism. The
words of the people of Capernaum, 'What is this? A new kind
of teaching! He speaks with authority' (Mark 1.27) concisely
expressed the Church's own developing self-awareness of
being rooted in, yet distinct from its Jewish environment.
Uncertainty about whether Jesus envisaged a wide-scale
mission to Gentiles, the variety of attitudes and practice in the
early Churches according to the Book of Acts, and the anxious
debate of Paul both with himself and with opponents about the
continuing significance of Jewish law both moral and ritual,
all testify to the centrality for the early Church of its ambiguous relationship with Judaism. Every topic of Christian
teaching has its antecedents in Judaism, whether official

* A good example of such a work is Rudolf Bultmann's, *Primitive
Christianity in its Contemporary Setting*, Fontana Library (London, 1960).
† Outstanding still are C. G. Montefiore's two volumes, *The Synoptic
Gospels* (London, 1927), first edition published in 1907. See also, S.
Sandmel, *We Jews and Jesus* (London, 1965).

orthodoxy or in one of the many forms of heterodoxy which also flourished. And the distinctiveness of every topic of Christian teaching originally derives from those early debates in which the new Christian synagogues sought to clarify their position in relation to the traditions of the Old Testament. The presence of Gentiles, and the need for their instruction in the new way, also helped to bring the faith to a more precise definition of itself.

In the middle of this development, which undoubtedly proceeded at different paces in different parts of the Roman Empire, the New Testament documents were written. The earliest letter, probably 1 Thessalonians, was most likely written within twenty years of the crucifixion of Jesus; and the earliest gospel, probably Mark, within forty years. The precise dates are often impossible to determine with certainty, and in the case of 2 Peter (often thought to be the latest document) competent scholars have offered dates, varying between AD 60 and AD 140. Bearing in mind the variety of dates, provenances, purposes and authors of the documents, and the fact that they wrote within the middle of a critical process of development, what *ought* to astonish the reader (had he not been otherwise conditioned) is the impressive unity of the collection. Having been told, however, virtually from the cradle, of the unity of the New Testament (with the possible corollary of its infallibility), the modern Christian reader may be inclined to find its variety slightly shocking. The business of contrasting Paul with James, or John with the writers of the Synoptic Gospels acquires an aura of daring scepticism, with the consequence that mountains of contradiction are made out of molehills of divergent emphasis. In fact, of course, a very great deal of the impression which the documents may make on us turns upon the eyes with which we read them; and it may require a considerable effort to see them as the documents they were intended to be, rather than the 'Holy', and rather remote, Scripture which the Church has made out of them.

These, then, are our various witnesses to Jesus; what do they contain? If we study the content of the New Testament witness to Jesus we see that it falls into four main categories; (i) the reported teaching and ministry of Jesus himself, (ii) the facts of his death and their interpretation, (iii) the claims, both historical and existential, for his resurrection, and (iv) the continuing 'body' of Christ, the sacramental and ethical community. Each of these categories of material deserve to be studied in detail, but there is something to be said for investigating in a deliberately broad and outline way the historical considerations which they respectively raise.

We ask, then, the obvious question concerning the narratives of the New Testament, How reliable may we suppose them to be?

It is not perhaps to the credit of theologians that one needs to say that this is a perfectly proper question. Some sophisticated attempts have been made so to blend history and interpretation, that the commonsense question of facticity—whether something 'actually happened'—disappears in a blur of personal view-point. History, however, requires this commonsense approach, and validates the obvious distinction between a fact and a fable, whatever sophistication may subsequently be necessary to unravel the nature of 'fact'. We cannot turn aside from the commonsense question of whether what is reported in the gospels and Acts is fact or fable even if we may have excruciating difficulty in giving satisfactory answers.

In order to give our answers, we manifestly need the disciplined and dispassionate approach of the professional historian. The question of reliability is, in principle, askable of any ancient document and requires to be answered with the identical, public standards of critical impartiality and integrity.

At the same time, precisely in order to achieve such standards, scholars of the New Testament are aware of important factors which disturb the normal equilibrium.

In the first place, in the case of Christians studying the New Testament, it must be stated that what is there recorded may well be a matter of consuming interest to their own personal faith. May this not mean that they will 'twist' the facts to suit their convictions? It would, of course, be ludicrous to insist that only those who are deeply bored by and indifferent to the literature they study are capable of an impartial view of it. But the 'interest' of Christians in the New Testament may have both of two consequences. Helpfully, it may attune their sensitivities to the nuances of meaning which the literature conveys; but also, unhelpfully, it may predispose their minds to adopt noncritical attitudes where critical judgements would have been illuminating. The Christian literature of the centuries has abundant illustrations of both the uncritical and, more recently and by compensation, the hypercritical mentality. There is, of course, also anti-Christian literature of a biased type with a dishonest investment in negative answers to historical questions. But after two centuries of the most searchingly critical investigation, the New Testament scholar is quite prepared to face all the implications of the public question of the substantial reliability of the documents, and to give his answers in a manner which reflects the common ground between believer and non-believer in this area.

But secondly, he will recognise that much will depend upon the attitude which the historian takes up towards miracle stories. A good deal of the New Testament reports events of a supernatural character. What attitude can the impartial historian take towards miracle stories in his documents? The answer may be that he is neither obliged to be credulous, nor to seek to disprove them. He will naturally want to take cognisance of the quality of the literature in which they occur.

In the case of the gospels this will involve bearing in mind both the importance that the accurate testimony of history and of fact had for early Christians, and the fact that the gospels and Acts were written by believers to bear witness to the power of Christ. But he will also need to consider the role of the miracle story in world literature, and the philosophical function of the term in religious discourse. Such considerations, which are long overdue in modern theology, will need to be brought together and weighed; and it must be recognised that a considerable amount depends upon the final verdict.* For if the miracle stories of the gospels are felt to be examples of the legend-making mentality of emotionally excited men, then much of the New Testament, including the resurrection of Jesus, will be rejected as unreliable. If, on the other hand, no good reasons exist for doubting in principle the reports of the New Testament, it becomes permissible to reflect on the nature of the *dynamis*, or power, which was said to go forth from Jesus, and to take individually and with complete seriousness the reports of his miraculous activities.

A final difficulty which disturbs the scholar who seeks to study the New Testament with dispassion and impartiality is the relative absence of corroborative material. Only the existence, the death and reports of the alleged resurrection of Jesus could be said to receive independent corroboration. And we are tantalisingly deficient in our evidence for the detailed internal development of the Church in the first century. Only the book of Acts (scholars place the date of composition between AD 70 and AD 130; most frequently, AD 85) records extracts from the story of parts of the Church up to the death of Paul, which are partially substantiated by Paul's own letters. The period from the crucifixion to AD 70 can only be conjecturally reconstructed; and the difficulty is that upon the

* See, C. F. D. Moule (ed.), *Miracles*, Cambridge Studies in their Philosophy and History (London, 1965).

F

results of the conjectural reconstruction a good deal depends. For either the reports of the teaching and ministry of Jesus were preserved relatively unimpaired during those forty years, in which case we can take the gospels much as they stand, or a complex process of development altered and adapted the teaching to make it relevant to new situations.

How did the Church preserve the teaching of Jesus, and how did the gospels come to be written? In order to answer this question the historical scholar is obliged to formulate a theory on the basis of the major elements of the evidence, and then to test the theory against each individual section of the gospel. A hundred years ago it was often held that Mark was the first gospel to be written, that Matthew and Luke combined with Mark a source of sayings of Jesus common to them both, and that John was a more or less free composition of the evangelist. The uncertainty of the criteria for the hypotheses is well illustrated by the fact that not even today can these views be regarded as 'results' of criticism. Although the material has been more extensively analysed and studied than almost any other body of literature of comparable size, the only fact of which we may be assured is that the conclusions are provisional.

All these three factors, the deep concern of the Christian, the difficulty for historical study of the supernatural, and the paucity of corroborative material tend to disturb the studied equilibrium of the impartial scholar who works on the records of the teaching and ministry of Jesus. The result is twofold: every critical description of that teaching and ministry will be based on a reconstruction and certain conjectures which will only be to varying degrees verifiable; and there will be present an inescapable element of personal reaction. This conclusion is important in that it helps to explain the otherwise bewildering variety of scholarly writing about Jesus; and it should serve as a warning to both writer and reader not to attach too great importance to the 'conclusions' of any such study.

It will not have escaped the attentive reader that the Christian faith is thus presented with an acute dilemma. It insists that its doctrine is based on something that 'actually happened', an individual life and its effect on others, and yet at the same time it is unable to say with any scholarly precision exactly *what* happened. Even the scholar who wishes to reconstruct the story quite dispassionately is forced in the end to make judgements which may rest upon philosophical or religious grounds. His only alternative will be constantly to return an open verdict, saying in effect that one must remain agnostic because of insufficient evidence either way.

As I have mentioned, the history of Jesus presents us with considerable elements of the supernatural in the form of miracles. In point of fact, however, the whole 'event' of Jesus is said to be divine activity; God sent his Son, he raised him from the dead. One could only understand what had 'actually happened' if one set the whole life, death and resurrection of Jesus in the context of 'the deliberate will and plan of God', according to the early Christians (Acts 2.23). It is at this point that history and theology intertwine in a bewildering way. For it is impossible to separate them by calling the theology an 'interpretation' of what 'actually happened'. For what had 'actually happened' according to the early Christians was that God had acted in the history of Jesus.

It is the construing of this statement which has provided Christian theology with its principal task for nineteen hundred years. In some ages it has seemed most important to know precisely the relationship between God and Jesus; in others, again, how God's activity in Jesus relates to his other activities. But at the base of these inquiries has lain the question of God's person and nature. How do we understand God to be and what is the meaning of God acting? Anyone who wishes to know whether it is true that what 'actually happened' in the history of Jesus was that God sent his Son, is immediately involved in both these questions. It is impossible to read the New Testament and to ignore them.

The only way to approach the question is by inquiring what else it is that God is said to have done. It will be seen at once that God's activities are not supposed to preclude natural agencies. God is said to have brought out the people of Israel from Egypt, though Moses was manifestly a leader. Furthermore these activities have perfectly perceptible outcomes. When God is said to have healed, a perceptible change results. Thus the statement lends itself to a total disproof, if after the alleged healing the symptoms are still fully manifest. Nothing can be said to have been 'done' by God, which has been disproved in this way. One further characteristic of alleged activities of God is that fallible and imperfect human elements may be included in the total act. God may thus not be manifest in every feature of the activity, nor need the activity exhaust the depth of any aspect of his nature.

So when it is said that God 'acted' in the history of Jesus, there remains a very great deal of further thought to be given. What is said is that the whole of a personal life was a perceptible outcome of the activity of God. For the early Christians this very clearly placed Jesus in a category by himself, for which the best adjective that John could find was 'only-begotten', which he used in his crucial sentence, 'God loved the world so much that he gave his only Son' (John 3.16). By this adjective Jesus is distinguished from those other children of God, who also are sent by God to do a particular task in the world and are also part of his activity. But despite this important distinction there is no need to grasp at every available superlative. We may quite properly pursue the questions outlined above about the activity of God. It remains the distinctive Christian witness to Jesus that of no other

individual can it be said that the whole of his history was the
activity of God. But this need not mean either that every
single element of that activity manifested the whole nature of
God, or that any element of it exhaustively manifested the
depth of any aspect of God. The early Church worried deeply
about this question, since it seemed inappropriate to them
that God's only Son should need to eat and drink. We may
believe, quite consistently, that what stands before us as the
biblical witness to Jesus is both a paradigm of the relations of
God and the world, and yet is not an exhaustive revelation of
God. That is to say, taking the gospel records as a whole we
may believe that nowhere else do we have clearer knowledge of
the nature and quality of God's dealings with man; and at the
same time we need not suppose that every story reveals its
extent, nor even that we *only* know of God's activity by the
gospel records.

We need, now, to draw this discussion together by inquiring
what kind of writing about Jesus of Nazareth we may expect
from theologians today. First of all, as this chapter will have
made abundantly clear, we must expect a rigorously critical
exposition of the historical problems of the New Testament
records. If the Christian faith wishes to reap the advantages of
being based in the actual life-history of an individual, it must be
prepared to face the dangers. The problem of the resurrection
is a case in point. Some at least of the New Testament writers
believed that Jesus left the tomb where he had been buried, a
claim subject to disproof by the production of a corpse. A
modern treatment of the subject of the resurrection cannot
lightly pass over the various types of difficulties in this testimony, nor should the Christian faith lightly swap its belief in
the empty tomb for a more 'spiritual' account of the liberating
force of belief in a metaphorically 'risen' Lord.* Statements

* See the fascinating discussion by G. W. H. Lampe and D. M.
MacKinnon in *The Resurrection*, ed. W. Purcell (London, 1966), and the

about what God has done in a perceptible way certainly lend themselves to *dis*proof, but not, of course, to proof. Even if it were to be shown that the body of Jesus left the tomb, it still would not follow that *God* had raised him from the dead. But disappointment that dispassionate historical study cannot confirm our theology for us should not allow theologians to ignore the importance of historical investigations for what they say about Jesus. And we may legitimately hope for a de-escalation of superlatives as a result of such studies. The full force of the originality of the history of Jesus can stand on its own, unadorned by a dressing of apologetic froth.

But secondly we may expect from theologians some genuinely original evaluations of the significance of Jesus in the context of the activity of God. The significance of Jesus was interpreted by the early Christians in the light of what they believed to be the activity of God in the history of Israel. Our view may easily be wider than that; it will most certainly be different. For we have a different view of how God acted, for example, in the creation of the world and of man. While the stories of the gospels remain paradigmatic for the relations of God and the world, the theological context in which we set these stories has altered.

Finally, one may hope for a more persuasive use of the significance of the fact of Jesus for the Christian religion. Even bearing all the historical problems in mind, and the probable variety of verdicts and reconstructions, the fact that the centre of the faith is an event rather than an idea is of paramount importance. The Christian believes that something 'actually happened'. What he believes is certainly open to disproof; should it be true, however, it has a quality, which no idea, no matter how persuasive, can possibly possess. He believes that

collection of essays by German theologians, *The Significance of the Message of the Resurrection for Faith in Jesus Christ*, edited, with an introduction, by C. F. D. Moule (London, 1968).

God takes the kind of interest in the world and its ambiguous and tragic history which leads to certain perceptible and factual results. His faith is thus fully capable of coping with human realities. It is not a rarified pietism nor starry-eyed idealism. Anything that smacks of illusion or self-deception is repugnant to it. And all this follows from the hard quality of God's love for man. If that love involves the ambiguities of birth, experience, family life and education, acceptance and rejection, betrayal, torture and public crucifixion, then the optimism of the resurrection and ascension is qualitatively altered. The Christian believes in the kingdom of God and in salvation through Christ on the basis of what has 'actually happened'. And he will look for this kingdom and this salvation not in a never-never world of his private imagination, but in concrete events and people. And it is precisely the concreteness of this hope that lies at the root of any persistence or effectiveness that he may possess.

6

CREATION AND GOD

In the last chapter attention was concentrated, rather narrowly it might be thought, upon Jesus. Many people are Christians, however, not primarily because of Jesus, but because they believe in God; God, indeed, as he is understood in the Christian religion, but not by any means confined to the one who acted in the person of Jesus of Nazareth. This form of the faith may be fully justified. It is probable that Jesus and God provide the Christian faith with two foci of separable significance. Some Christians concentrate more exclusively upon Jesus, and develop a deep, personal intimacy with the thought of the person of Christ which many of the most familiar hymns in the English language reflect (e.g. 'Jesu, lover of my soul' and 'Jesu, the very thought of thee', a translation of an eleventh-century hymn). On the other hand, Christian faith also encourages the wider vision of God as creator and sustainer of all that is and many Christians concentrate on the way in which Christian life and thought is a fulfilment of the order and purpose evident in creation. The classic position in theology is that these two foci are fully united in the interpenetration of the themes of creation and redemption, as they are most beautifully in the General Thanksgiving in the Book of Common Prayer.

But the two points of focus probably are psychologically, rather than theologically, divergent. Theology must naturally present and preserve them both in due perspective, in order to avoid imbalance. But Christians may well find themselves instinctively drawn to one of them, at least initially, while finding the other to be rather troublesome. Thus those who tend to concentrate upon Jesus sometimes regard the wider view as optional intellectual speculation, and their own perspective as 'real' or 'personal' faith; while those who prefer the wider view occasionally speak scornfully of the 'Jesus-cult' and 'hot-house' religion. This tendency to divide into two camps, evident even before the Reformation, received added impetus from the divisions then created and the subsequent divisions of the Enlightenment. Thus interest in Jesus has remained strong where critical procedures have yielded firm knowledge of his life and teaching; whereas more sceptical attitudes have led to a devaluation of the supernatural and even a unitarian doctrine of the Godhead. Even these divisions, however, are largely being overcome in the more recent movements of theology.

At the same time an interesting relic from the past may be evident in the current structure of philosophical discussions between Christians and agnostics or atheists. A celebrated work appearing in 1955, entitled *New Essays in Philosophical Theology*,* inaugurated amongst philosophers a debate about questions of belief in God which has been of considerable interest to theologians. But it is typical that much of this debate is about God as he might have been conceived by eighteenth-century philosophy; that is to say, indubitably the God of classic Christian theism, but without the consideration of the specific difference which believing in Christ makes to the structure of that belief.† It may be thought possible by philosophers to discuss the 'broad' question of God, without

* London, ed. A. Flew and A. Macintyre. It should be said that the views of the contributors have in a number of instances altered considerably since 1955.

† A significant recognition of the need to consider Christ occurs in the discussion of Creation by A. Flew and D. M. MacKinnon, pp. 170–86, but in the penultimate paragraph!

it being necessary to get down to 'details' in the person of Christ. It will, however, be the aim of this present discussion to keep the Christian's fundamental orientation towards Jesus at the centre of the attempt to answer the questions which arise from speaking of creation.

What then is meant by the word 'creation'? It is in itself an interesting word, since common usage tends to reserve it for imaginative mental activity. Even in *haute couture* a Paris 'creation' is a way of referring to French genius for the styling of clothes, rather than for the technical work of tailoring. We use the word creative when we want to call attention to the element of novelty in a person's imaginative capacities. At the same time experience shows that even in highly creative achievements there are borrowed elements. The mind works upon pre-existing material from its life-experience, which inevitably precludes absolute novelty of imagination. In the end the only way we can give meaning to the concept of unique novelty is the disappointing notion that a thing is what it is and nothing else. Even my mass-produced ball-point pen is unique in that sense.

A creation, then, in our ordinary use of the term is a novel imaginative achievement, and generally one upon which we set high value. The first point to be made about the sense of the word creation in Christian theology is that the Christian means that all-that-is is part of the purposive activity of God. It is God's imaginative achievement. Having said that, we have, of course evoked the image of an artist of genius who produces ideas for some novel activity of the spirit. And the more concrete our image of the artist becomes, the more we realise that in many important respects God is unlike him. The life-experience of the artist, for example, which enables us to set his achievements in time and space, has no parallel in God. In what sense could everything-that-is be an achievement of a previous life-experience in God? It becomes very quickly obvious that the whole concept of experience has meaning only in the context of time.

This is precisely the problem with the concept of creation, that nothing which we could conceive could possibly be adequate to the proposal that all-that-is came about as a result of creative activity. The (at first sight) so plausible idea that causally we should be able to trace back everything to the point of creation by God turns out to arrive at a paradox. To say that God created all-that-is is to use language which apparently requires that something existed 'before' creation. We simply have no way of proposing to ourselves an absolute beginning of everything.

It is when we are driven up against a logical wall like this that it is important to recall the Christian context of the concept of creation. Its context is that of God's purpose for and over-sight of creation. When, in the teaching of Jesus, God is spoken of as clothing the grass or caring for sparrows, it is in the context of encouragement not to be anxious but to set one's mind on God's kingdom. For to live in the kingdom is to live out God's purpose for oneself. It is not so much to be con-scious in great detail that one's life is fulfilling God's purposes, as to be assured of the overall orientation of one's life and to be freed from the anxiety of supposing that life has no meaning. That is to say, the idea of the creation of all-that-is by God functions in the Christian faith as an assurance against the threat of meaninglessness. Whether it has further ramifications is a question to which we must return; but for the moment we can dwell on this existential side of the idea of creation.

In emphasising assurance as a function of the idea of crea-tion, the Christian immediately exposes himself to the charge of wishful thinking. He is told that so incoherent an idea as an original creation of all-that-is by God could only continue to exist if it served some devious psychological purpose, for example as a bolster against despair. This kind of objection is familiar. But the fact that a religious belief may serve a psychological need can never be in itself sufficient evidence that it is derived from that need. The Christian can freely admit the existence of the need for reassurance against the threat of meaninglessness. He may himself have experienced at one time or another a paralysing sense of futility on facing the fact that there is no self-evident reason why he, as an individual, should be aware of his own existence, but that inanimate objects should apparently not be. These disturbing thoughts, while not necessarily common, are none the less well documented, particularly in the literature of the twentieth century.

In point of fact an individual is not bound to have to face the threat of meaninglessness or futility at all. The society in which the individual lives provides protection against such disturbances and teaches him in various practical ways that his life has certain particular purposes. By education and social pressures it encourages him to adopt a certain rôle. It influences his expectations of his working and family life, and if he fits into the pattern laid down he is expected to live out a happy existence. This is by no means as Machiavellian as it sounds. The existence of social norms to guide behaviour promotes order and mental stability and protects man from time-wasting consideration of every slightest action, though it may also make him incapable of viewing his society critically and rob him of the freedom to engage in new enterprises.

In the Western world today we are still in a period where elements of the Christian understanding of the purpose of man effectively determine the social norms. The evidence of conflict is also very marked, where these norms are being challenged. Commonly we categorize these latter as *ethical* dilemmas of our era, for instance, as questions of sexual morality and the morality of capitalism. But their real root is whether we have any confidence that our searchings for the purpose of existence, and thus for the purpose of the sexual instinct or of technical skills, yields us any normative answers. The practical need for answers to these questions is considerable, and overtakes academic theorising about whether we create purposes for ourselves for psychological reasons. The knowledge that we have a psychological need to express purpose in our lives does not free us from that need. The question is not whether one will have a purpose or no, but what purpose one has. And this question turns upon the *basis* upon which that purpose is built. How does one arrive at a purpose for one's life?

At this point in the discussion it would be possible to turn in either of two directions. We have seen that part of what the Christian means when he has spoken of the creation by God of the world is that the world has a purpose. We have seen how practically important the purpose question is for man. It would now be possible to build a link with Jesus by speaking of the way in which discipleship of Jesus, both following his own teaching and meditating upon his significance, provides an individual with a clear purpose.

But this would not at all be how many people would follow up the question of the value man gives to his own existence in its natural environment. For them the question could first be a scientific one. What is man in his environment? Does not a descriptive account of man yield us the necessary clues to all the important practical matters of purpose which we may like to raise? The divergence is significant. For the term 'creation' has both the theological-existential and the scientific-factual side to it. At one time it may have been thought that the book of Genesis decided not merely the former questions but also the latter. Nowadays, those who speak of creation may well be referring solely to scientific theories of the origins of the universe, which they would justify solely by empirical observations. And many recent books about man, which do not hesitate to make recommendations in the sphere of morals, believe that they do so solely on the basis of a descriptive account of man as one part of the animal kingdom.

The parting of the ways of these two methods is of the deepest significance for Christian theology. For theology appears to have to decide whether its statements about creation have any empirical consequences; whether, that is, what it claims to know about the purpose of existence results in statements which might be *dis*proved by scientific investigation. Those who wish to avoid this question understand Christianity as a way of giving meaning to existence which is not necessarily inherent in existence itself. They point to the disastrous record of Christian dogmatic interference in scientific inquiry, and its frequent retreats from untenable positions. They draw the consequence that religious faith and scientific research are totally distinguishable forms of activity. In theology this attitude results in confining the meaning of the idea of creation to those existential questions of purpose and meaning which we have just examined.

But once again, as with the discussion of the significance of history, Christianity cannot reap the advantages of claiming to be involved with reality without being prepared to face the dangers. The activity of God in Jesus Christ is as much an activity in nature as it is in history. If the faith is based on this activity it is open both to historical and to 'natural' investigation. For Jesus Christ occupies both time and space; and as the paradigm of God's activity we may properly subject him to the scrutiny appropriate to observation in these fields. The inclination of modern study to turn to the scientific study of man in his environment to understand his purpose seems entirely justified *from the standpoint of Christian faith itself.*

We return therefore to the commonsense question, Where does everything come from? We have noticed that this is a very special question, only apparently similar to the question, Where does this or that come from? To ask where everything comes from is not merely to ask what caused the first elementary particle; it is to ask what is the basis of the whole of our ability to perceive things as entities in time and space. And this is the question that is at once raised when we try to form the notion of a 'beginning of time'. The fact is that we simply do not know whether everything that exists originates from such a beginning. Scientists who are prepared to use their imaginations offer us various guesses, which are partly subject to disproof by empirical observation. But there is no agreement either on whether the world is finite or infinite, or on whether we can speak sensibly of a beginning of time at all.

But from these disappointingly uncertain conclusions a recent writer on science and religion draws a very positive moral. Referring to the possibility that the whole of our framework of space and time may have to be abandoned in order to resolve the current confusion in physics, he concludes:

> For these reasons alone, it would be quite profitless to speculate on the purpose behind the existence of matter, or the purpose behind the universe as a whole. . . . It would not be inconsistent if the universe itself were to be an effect for which there is no specific cause.*

The same conclusion frequently emerges in discussions with agnostics and atheists who allege scientific grounds for their beliefs. If scientific investigation does not itself indubitably assure us that the existence of matter shows signs of its own purpose, they assert, then speculation about possible purposes is a waste of time. But this is surely not the case. For it is precisely the function of speculation, and of the use of imagination in science, to provide theses which may be tested by

* Alan Isaacs, *The Survival of God in the Scientific Age* (Harmondsworth, 1966), p. 36. This book argues that belief in God is not based on any evidence which does not lend itself to a more rational, or at least, an alternative explanation.

observation. Why, in the name of science, should one dogmatically assert that it is 'quite profitless' to launch on the most daring enterprise of all, a hypothesis to explain why everything-that-is exists at all? Many writers have remarked upon the existence of scientific obscurantism when scientists come to consider phenomena in the physical world which might upset their current picture of the world, for example in medicine or psychical research. But we should also notice the dotty 'alchemist' fringe which loiters on the borderlands of science, and which is constantly attracted by speculation. One can scarcely blame a busy scientist for refusing to spend time upon possibly profitless activity, when so much of a solid nature remains to be done. This, however, does not invalidate the contention. It is one thing for a scientist to be too busy to engage in speculation over the whole field; it is quite another thing for a scientific journalist to declare all such speculation to be 'quite profitless'. In the one case it is a perfectly proper but quite individual question of the apportionment of time and effort; in the other case it is an apparent refusal to admit that such speculation ever could serve a constructive end.

And here we must mention one particularly daring act of speculative thesis-formation, by the notable French palaeontologist, Père Pierre Teilhard de Chardin (1881-1955). According to Teilhard, matter inherently contains within itself the tendency to organize itself into an increasingly complex mass, and to develop in the direction of consciousness. This 'Law of Complexity-Consciousness', as it is called, he does not hesitate to describe as the purpose which matter exhibits; and as a Catholic theologian he is naturally prepared to speak, on a transexperiential plane, of God taking shape within matter and of Christ as the first-born of all creation. Needless to say these speculations are highly controversial to scientists. For the publication in English of *Le Phenomène*

G

Humain in 1959* Sir Julian Huxley, the eminent biologist, contributed an introduction in which he wrote:

> Though many scientists may, as I do, find it impossible to follow him all the way in his gallant attempt to reconcile the supernatural elements in Christianity with the facts and implications of evolution, this in no way detracts from the positive value of his approach.†

On the other hand, P. B. Medawar in a highly critical review published in *Mind* in January, 1961, attacked both Teilhard and Huxley for their 'gullibility' and seemed angered that the book should pass as a scientific treatise. On reflection, he was later prepared to agree that there was no real harm in its 'dotty, euphoristic kind of nonsense', and himself to argue strongly for the use of imagination in scientific work.‡ Scientists continue to disagree about the significance of his work, which certainly suffered through not being exposed to learned criticism during his life-time. But the importance of Teilhard is not merely that he proposed his particular theory in his own special vocabulary; it is, rather, that the attempt was made by a scientist to look at the world as a whole, and to offer an interpretation of its meaning which might be subjected to scientific criticism. This constitutes a rather striking form of openmindedness, and contrasts with the attitude which designates all attempt at synthesis as 'quite profitless'. It is a healthy reversal of affairs which reveals a Christian in the position of opening up horizons in the domain of the scientific study of man.

The reason for this, at first sight, rather curious fact is that a Christian's faith in God demands of him some conception of

* Teilhard completed this work in 1940. In 1944 permission to publish it was refused by Rome, and the work did not appear until 1955, posthumously.

† *The Phenomenon of Man* (London, 1965), p. 20.

‡ *The Art of the Soluble* (London, 1967), p. 9 and pp. 131 ff.

the relation of God and the world, and enables him to keep an open mind when he reaches the apparent boundaries of perception. When it is clearly understood that it is only by imagination that any concept of creation can be framed at all, the activity of a scientist making a guess about the origins of the universe, or its purpose, is not greatly dissimilar from that of a Christian theologian trying to explain what he means by speaking of God's creative purpose. This is not to say that they do not speak on the basis of different commitments. The scientist is compelled to say something because the world is there and calls for some explanation. The theologian, who also faces the reality of the world, believes that God loves that world and has acted in it. Of this activity he already has some experience, and he wishes to use his present insights as an aid to his imagination in framing a conception of how God and the world are related. But, in so doing, the theologian is bound to expose his statements to scientific disproof; the only alternative is to use language which cannot be shown in any way to be more or less probably true.

If the Christian theologian is prepared to risk disproof by empirical methods, all his positive statements on creation are going to be of a more or less provisional character. Is this a tolerable position for him to occupy? Is he not involved in changing his view every other year? And what becomes of the stability of his discipline, not to mention the stability of his faith? These questions are extremely important, and they have a similar structure to the questions about history which occupied us in the previous chapter.

But once again the situation is far from hopeless. It must be granted that the theological contributions to the subject of creation are bound to be pluriform, rather than uniform; there will be no single, authoritative 'doctrine of creation'. But all contributions will contain a common reference point in the witness to the paradigmatic act of God in Jesus Christ. That is to say, the quality or character of God's dealings with the world became evident in the divine participation in the human condition. The witnesses to that event of participation raise in a positive way the issues of time and eternity, of the world and God, which are the subject matter of all theological talk about creation. In his careful attention to the biblical witness to Jesus, the theologian has a stable subject matter which provides the continuity for his discipline.

But to this discipline he must be allowed to bring both the most recent scientific knowledge about man and the environment in which he lives, and also gifts of imagination and insight essential to any creative work. And this will necessarily mean that his conclusions will be of a provisional character. I do not believe this to be a disadvantage in the long run, though it will make it difficult for the layman to be abreast of current research. It will also require a particular species of courage to make his speculations public and subject to the quality of criticism evident in, for example, Medawar's review of Teilhard. But there is considerable gain, particularly if Christians can be relied upon to provide those attempts at synthesis which alone can prevent scientific research and human thought from degenerating into a collection of unrelated and narrow specialisms. For only such syntheses, which require enormous gifts both of outlook and of general knowledge, give hope of answers to the questions of purpose and meaning which press in upon us in our practical affairs.

We are now in a position to answer directly the question with which this chapter opened, namely, How do we so understand the significance of Jesus that he begins to answer the questions which arise when we consider the nature and purpose of the universe? We reply that we understand Jesus to be a paradigm of the activity of God. Those who wish to say anything at all about the activity of God have nothing better to point to than the whole life of Jesus of Nazareth; not that there is no other activity, nor that in any given act of Jesus the whole nature of God is manifest, but that as a whole the event of Jesus' life is an unparalleled model of God's relations with the world. Whatever we say about God must therefore be visible in some aspect of the event of Jesus. But because that event is subject to both historical and 'natural' scrutiny it is not possible to use any aspect whatsoever to justify what one says about God. One cannot, for example, appeal without discussion to the report of the empty tomb to validate one particular account of the relations of natural and supernatural in the realm of physical nature. But in the course of any statements about God's activities there will be a necessary reference to the event of Jesus as it is recorded by the biblical witness and as studied by modern scholars. Nothing less than such a reference could establish the person of Jesus as paradigmatic for the activity of God.

But there is a second aspect of the significance of Jesus for these questions. This is the existential significance for the individual, whose practical interest in the nature and destiny of the universe is how he may orient his own life. The experience of being a creature contributes to the importance which men attach to discussion of their origins, and cannot be avoided in merely scholarly or abstruse speculation. The Christian believes that the life of discipleship on which he has embarked consists in a radical orientation of his whole being upon the person of his Lord and Master. As with any other all-embracing and all-absorbing discipleship, the personality is unified about a single centre. In this straightforward psychological sense the activity of discipleship is an important contribution to mental stability. But the Christian's claims are more far-reaching than this. He believes that the themes of discipleship which form the content of Christian faith are essential to living, and that without them any life is impoverished. This claim turns upon the particular quality of love which he trusts may be evident in his behaviour, and that love, in turn, depends upon his reflection of the love of his Lord. Such a love, he believes, expresses, as nothing else, the purpose of all existence. Thus the significance of Jesus is, that of the one who gives concrete meaning to individual existence, who orientates the creative potential of each human being and who enriches their life-experience of love.

7
'OTHER RELIGIONS' AND CHRISTIANITY

IN considering the attitude of Christianity to 'other religions', there are two facts of paramount importance; first, that the vast preponderance of humanity have not in any way been reached or effectively influenced by Christian faith; secondly, that there is the closest possible relationship between any given society and the religion it professes. Both of these facts are used as arguments against the universal validity of Christianity, and the latter may be used against the finality of *any* religion. We observe that many religions claim to possess the final key to the riddle of life; but is any one of these claims likely to be true, given all the facts of cultural diversity of which we are aware? Doubtless if one had been born in a Moslem country one would have been a Moslem; and so on. The argument is familiar, and the facts are not in dispute. But what is disputed is the correct inference to draw from these facts.

This is not the place to consider the history of the process whereby Christianity has been brought to consider more carefully the significance of 'other religions'.* Certainly one landmark was the work of Lord Herbert of Cherbury (1583–1648), who attempted to state the five 'common notions' upon which every religion is founded; 'if we set aside superstitions and legends, the mind takes its stand on my five articles, and

* See E. L. Allen, *Christianity among the Religions* (London, 1960).

upon nothing else'.* Lord Herbert's work did much to stimulate the writers of the late seventeenth and early eighteenth centuries both in Britain and on the Continent. It had two principle points to make; the first, that religion manifested itself in great variety and, secondly, that one might usefully distinguish between what was *natural* to all men, and what was said to be *revealed* to only a few. The implication of this second point was clearly that natural religion was more certainly true than allegedly revealed religion, and the Deists of the late seventeenth and early eighteenth centuries did not hesitate to go beyond Lord Herbert by developing an explicit critique of the so-called divine revelations.

The real impact of this line of criticism was not, however, apparent until historical study of the books of the Bible began to reveal that the Christian's records of divine revelation themselves had a history. When it became clear that early Christianity had developed in ways which might be reconstructed by historical criticism, the case against the finality of Christian revelation seemed to be immensely strengthened. The sophisticated writers of the French and German enlightenment felt that revealed religion would soon disappear once its fraudulant claims to divine authority had been exposed.

That Christianity has now faced these criticisms for 200 years is itself a remarkable fact. During this period a number of highly significant developments have taken place, including the great missionary activity of the nineteenth century, two world wars, and the inventions of radio and of air travel which have revolutionised world communications. But important though these developments are in bringing the problem of the relation of Christianity to 'other religions' to the forefront of theological debate, the challenge which the Christian faith faces to authenticate its claim to convey the final truth about God's activity has scarcely altered.

* *De Veritate*, tr. H. M. Carré (Bristol, 1937), p. 304.

Scarcely anyone has put the case which Christianity has to answer with more subtlety and imagination than Gotthold Ephraim Lessing (1729–81), one of the principal figures of the German enlightenment. Deeply interested in philosophy and theology he embarked on a literary career, expressing his views by editing the writings of an early German biblical critic, and in his plays. One of the latter, *Nathan the Wise* (1779), is so interesting for our purposes that it deserves extended notice. The play concerns representatives of the three religions, Judaism (represented by Nathan, a Merchant), Islam (represented by Saladin, a Sultan) and Christianity (represented by the Knight Templar). The play not merely embodies Lessing's plea for mutual toleration between the religions, but includes some interesting statements about their respective claims for divine revelation.

When Nathan is questioned by Saladin about which is the true religion, he replies with a story. There was a family in which inheritance was a right passed from father to son by possession of a ring, which had the magic power of making the owner loved by God and men. A father in this family had three sons, and being weak and unwilling to disappoint any of them had two perfect counterfeit rings made. The three rings were then given to the sons, privately, one to each. At his death each son naturally claimed the right of inheritance, and resorted to law. The judge's verdict was ambiguous. At first he suggested that, because none of the brothers was outstandingly loved by all the others, all three rings were counterfeit. But then he added his counsel, that, if they really wished to find the original ring, they had better seek by gentleness, love and devotion to bring to light its inner power. Perhaps then at a later date some much wiser judge might be able to decide between them.

There is no need to enter the complicated field of the interpretation of the parable in the context of Lessing's thought to see the main outlines of the dilemma. The judge's first suggestion that all three rings might have been counterfeit was not in fact true. But its significance is that from his standpoint in time he was unable to verify which of the claims to the estate was valid. His subsequent counsel, therefore, was a temporary expedient rather than a judicial judgement. He advised the sons to pay less attention to the legal rights and wrongs of their particular case than to the acts of kindness by which they might commend themselves to their fellow men and to a future judge.

Whether or not Lessing's other writings bear this interpretation out, it is certainly possible on the basis of the story to see that the fact that many religions claim to be the one true religion constitutes no final ground why one of those claims may not in fact be true. But the position of the man who wishes to establish a judicial criterion by which he may arbitrate between various claimants is undeniably complicated. From the standpoint of the religions there can be *no* higher criterion, because it would constitute a higher truth than that contained in the religion itself. The counsel of the judge is thus not a judicial arbitration. He clearly expects each son to continue to claim the sole right to inheritance. The counsel is in fact a way for the sons to reach a *modus vivendi* with each other, and for them to establish their claims before some future and wiser judge than himself.

Some writers, taking Lessing's hostility to the orthodoxy of his day at its face value, have too hastily assumed that this play is simply a reiteration of the conventional view of the enlightenment that all the religions are equally true to those who believe them, and none of them any substitute for the basic, 'natural' religion of love and brotherhood. Without entering the complicated field of the extent to which Lessing ever fully expressed his own views, it is still possible to see in the parable an implicit criticism of the view which has come to be known as indifferentism, the refusal on the grounds of tolerance to distinguish between the differing claims of the religions. The parable of the ring definitely asserts both that one of the rings is genuine and that in the end it will become clear which brother possesses it. It is also clear that the true ring has a power which may be brought forth by the appropriate activity on the wearer's behalf. The agnosticism of the parable lies simply in the fact that no *neutral* observer of the rings and the brothers is in a position to make a judicial arbitration between them.

It is true that in other parts of the play the themes of humane tolerance and brotherly love are constantly valued above the barriers artificially erected by the different religions. It is also true that Nathan offers no better reason for believing his own religion to be true than disinclination to doubt the good faith of his own forebears, and clearly expects neither the Moslem nor the Christian to be prepared to doubt theirs. But the parable itself does not give support to the popular eighteenth-century theory that the positive religions are an irrational mixture of superstitions and prohibitions suitable only for keeping the lower orders happy and in their place; and many of the criticisms of ecclesiastical dogmatism are scarcely more than what a modern theologian would recognise to be just. The most telling of these criticisms is the view, urged throughout the play, that the believer's convictions of the rightness of his own faith does not bestow upon him civil privileges (in the parable, represented by the inheritance), including the right to oppress those who do not believe as he does.

This interpretation of the parable contains some important points for the attitude of Christianity towards 'other religions'; certainly the relevance of the parable today is seen in the still commonly expressed view that each religion may contain a grain of truth and that it is indifferent by which route one travels, since the destination is one and the same. For from the standpoint of either Christianity, Judaism or Islam, this position is untenable. The judge's counsel in the parable was *not* that each religion should drop its claims to exclusiveness; quite the contrary. The claims to finality were to be explicitly retained. But they were to be tested at the bar of experience.

We may, therefore, usefully distinguish between various positions:

(i) between the claim that one's faith is a final revelation of God, and the further claim that such a status implies civil or even psychological privileges;

(ii) between the right to propagate one's faith, and the right to propagate it by any means;

(iii) between the view that there is true and false in religion, as in all other matters of human investigation, and the view that we already possess certainty on all matters of dispute in religion.

In each of these pairs there is a justifiable position and an unjustifiable extension of it. We turn now from Lessing's instructive parable to develop these contrasts briefly as they apply to the Christian faith itself in its relations with 'other religions'.

(i) *The claim to finality.* The important preliminary here is to recognise that it does not follow from the Christian's claim that his faith is true, that other religions or atheism should be denied the right to exist. This freedom of conscience has not always existed, and did not, indeed, entirely exist in Lessing's Germany. *Nathan* rightly exposes the disgraceful attitudes of much Christian canon law towards Jews—attitudes which have persisted into our own century. But it is now clear that the man who denies that Christianity is true, whether atheist or adherent of another faith, is not to be subject to harassment as either emotionally unstable or morally defective. The claim to finality has unquestionably been associated in the past with political and ideological imperialism; the first step in considering this claim today is to recognise that it can be distinguished from imperialism of every kind.

The question of what precisely it is that the Christian faith claims to be finally true, and the precise sense in which it is true, cannot be laid out in a few neat propositions. In the next chapter an attempt is made to exhibit something of the complex interrelation of historical, religious and moral claims for truth which Christians may want to make. But it can be at once stated that the assertion of the finality of the Christian faith by no means necessitates the bleak and bare denial of all the truth claims of all 'other religions'.

We may take an illustration from the gospel of John. In this gospel Jesus' claim to *be* the truth and to *speak* the truth is very fully brought out. In one passage, in words to Jewish disciples, Jesus asserts: 'If you dwell within the revelation I have brought, you are indeed my disciples; you shall know the truth, and the truth will set you free' (John 8.31, NEB). To be within the sphere of discipleship, to be thus 'dwelling in Christ', is to receive the promise of knowing the truth. The important thing is that the revelation is something that can be 'dwelt in' and that knowledge of it is knowledge of a deeply personal kind. For John, as for contemporary Christians, such knowledge includes knowledge of the teaching of Jesus; but it is more than teaching, or rather it is teaching which bears within it life-giving and liberating power.

The significance of this characteristic of Christianity is that it radically affects the Christian's attitude to the doctrines of his own faith. When he considers these in relation to the teachings of, for example, Judaism or Islam, it cannot merely be a matter for him of assessing competing and mutually contradicting statements. It is certainly the case that Christianity has a teaching content which, if it is true, is in parts in contradiction

with the teaching content of Judaism or Islam. But working
out the combination of agreements and disagreements between
the *statements* of differing religions would result, from the
Christian's point of view, in a series of artificial comparisons
of little value. The unique truth of Christ does not consist in
the letter of orthodox statements, but in the living relationship
of discipleship which binds the believer's life to his. To this
living relationship, which is precipitated and nourished by the
believer's constant reflection upon the event of Jesus, is
brought the whole of the individual's life-experience. Such
experience may well reflect encounter both with other faiths
and with non-religious ways of organising and giving meaning
to existence.

Thus within Christian discipleship there is a constant
dialogue with the whole of life-experience, in which 'other
religions' are, at least potentially, partners. Through such
human experiences the Christian will be aware that men seek
to understand the fundamental mysteries of human living; and
as he bears in mind the wide variety of approach within the
Christian faith itself, corresponding to the many racial,
cultural and psychological differences of mankind, he will cease
to see the critical process of unifying all experience under his
fundamental discipleship simply as a bare comparison of
doctrinal statements.

I have spoken of 'other religions' as sources of human
experience. But is this not explicitly to deny their claim to constitute valid knowledge of God? Not at all. The difficulty here
is of attempting to generalise about 'other religions', when only
consideration of particular religions is adequate. It would be as
misleading to assert that 'other religions' constitute a genuine
revelation of God, as to assert the contrary. For 'the religions'
are by no means a homogeneous phenomenon. There are
religions, indeed there are versions of the Christian religion,
which need to be energetically resisted. In saying this we need

only appeal to the example of Jesus in his denunciations of a contemporary perversion of Pharisaism. But despite the variety of religions, there is a helpful sense in which they can be regarded as part of human experience, every bit as much as rationality is. To embrace the Christian faith is not to abandon rational thought or reflection; no more is it to turn one's back on genuine human experience. We speak of rationality and many other abilities by which life is enriched as gifts of God, whose proper use is a fundamental human responsibility. Christians may, therefore, quite properly see the religious capacity of mankind as one way in which God has seen fit to enrich man's life. For faith in God in Christ does not require us to believe that God has acted only in Christ. We may therefore expect that the critical evaluation of other religions will be at the same time a means of deepening and enriching the quality of our own understanding of Christ.

We may take an example. Judaism is a faith with a natural relationship to Christianity. The tendency in studying it is to concentrate on the reasons why Jews reject the Christian's account of the significance of Jesus. Here there are, of course, propositional contradictions which cannot be concealed. At the same time a Christian student of living Judaism stands to learn considerably from the quality of the covenanted obedience of the Jew towards God and the constructive rôle of law in his ethics. Paradoxically here he may acquire a measure of freedom from the 'pharasaic' conventions which have come to dominate the practice of Christian ethics in the course of centuries.

This is but one illustration of the kind of way in which it may be justly claimed that Christianity is receptive to another, admittedly closely related, faith. The often contemptuous dismissal of 'other religions' by Christian writers of the past has become impossible for us today. The study of the living religions of mankind is a task which must be accorded a position of high honour in the studies relevant to Christian faith, as a means of deepening understanding and insight.

It is possible to add that not only Christianity, but also those religions which are studied, may have something to gain. Much as Christians have reason to be grateful for Jewish scholars of the New Testament, so it is possible that Christian students of other religions may contribute to their development. This seems particularly likely in as much as it is the Christian faith alone which has experienced the full force of the onslaught of modern materialism, and has passed through fires of more than 150 years of rationalist criticism. The results of this, which are still appearing throughout the Christian Church, may be communicated in the friendly dialogue of religions which could ensue from a Christian initiative. There are some signs that this is already under way.*

(ii) *Evangelism.* The basic question here concerns the means used in evangelism. Our century has become rightly aware of the dangers of propaganda and indoctrination as a result of much wartime experience. The result of this experience is the attempt to ensure the freedom of the means of mass communication from control by any one pressure group. For Christianity in Europe this has meant an often painful process of disengagement, both from positions of privilege in education and from powers of censorship—a process not altogether complete even now. But the fact remains that the duty of evangelism, which rests on the Christian by reason of the fact that he believes his faith to be true, does not permit him to require that he be allowed to evangelise by any means whatsoever.

* See P. Schneider, *Sweeter than Honey* (London, 1966), a study of the relations of Christianity and contemporary Judaism; R. Panikkar, *The Unknown Christ of Hinduism* (London, 1964) and K. Cragg, *The Call of the Minaret* (Oxford, 1956).

What does 'evangelism' mean? In the previous section, we spoke of 'other religions' as 'partners in a dialogue'. This popular expression is in grave danger of being used in a hypocritical manner in order to gloss over differences and disagreements. Partnership seems to imply that the partners are on an equal footing; but is Christianity really prepared to enter on dialogue on such terms? In one sense, clearly it is not prepared to accept equality, namely equality of truth. For Christianity, one religion is not as good as another. But, as we argued above, this does not have the negative corollaries of implying that 'other religions' should not be heard. The equality in dialogue which Christianity does accept is the equal right of one partner to command the painstaking attention of the other. The fact that a Christian may believe that his own faith is true does not relieve him of the responsibility of trying to understand the faith of another.

It is, of course, possible to attempt to turn one's readiness to listen to others itself into an instrument of evangelism. This would be as though one were saying, 'See how loving my own religion makes me towards you. Do you not think such a loving religion must be true?' The explosion of wrath which greeted the Second Vatican Council's ill-fated attempts at establishing more friendly relations with Jews by retrospectively exculpating them of deicide is one example of the suspicions which may be harboured. Paradoxically nothing but the frank recognition that evangelism still remains one of the Christian's primary tasks could allay these doubts. It is natural enough that evangelism should be regarded with suspicion. Quite apart from the fact that it has been, and still is, pursued with methods which deny the integrity of the human personality, the feeling that one is being asked radically to change one's views is bound to be regarded by the individual concerned as a threat to his stability. But unless a Christian is actually prepared to abandon his desire to communicate his faith and to

H

hope for the conversion of those who do not as yet embrace it, no alternative remains but to acknowledge that such is his ultimate desire and his hope. At the same time he will believe that much is to be gained by mutual understanding between those whose views differ. The replacing of misunderstanding, suspicion and intolerance by 'warmth of mutual affection' is in any case a requirement of his own faith, and if dialogue achieves nothing more then it will not have been in vain.

But there is another point in relation to evangelism which is both important and often overlooked. This is, that the assumption that the Christian occupies a position from which he can pass judgement upon 'other religions', as though they were 'also rans', is entirely inappropriate. We have here to deal with a mental attitude, in which the logic of the position is secondary. In fact the Christian believes that his faith affords him a privileged position; in logic the assumption of superiority ought naturally to follow with corresponding devaluation of all alternatives, a logic which Christian history has certainly seen pursued with appalling consequences. But the attitude of dependence upon God which the Christian faith cultivates totally precludes the assumption of superiority. For faith in Christ is a gift of God, without merit on the part of the recipient, and the faith bestows momentous responsibilities of service to others which must determine and predominate in the pattern of relationships with others. The Christian is forbidden the position of judge; his awareness is not that others are deficient in certain respects, but that his faith is at their disposal. Evangelism springs from the positive value of his own faith rather than from the negative judgement of the belief of others. All he is prepared to say on the score of the final future destiny of others is that God's judgement is perfect and his mercy infinite.

We must face the question whether this does not rob

evangelism of one of its main motivations, namely fear for the safety of others. After all, it is said, if you saw a blind man walking over a cliff would you not do everything in your power to rescue him before it is too late? Indeed you would! You would advise, warn, cajole, pester, bully, deceive and even disable him, if it were necessary and if he were finally convinced no such cliff existed. And Christian history with its Inquisition, witch trials and evangelistic methods of emotional blackmail amply demonstrate the precise and disastrous force of this particular analogy.

The problem is not a modern one. It has always been known that means existed for making people change their religious allegiance, of which fear has been the principal one in the past. If one thinks that those who do not confess Christian faith are in eternal danger, whether or not one uses gross methods in order to frighten them, the fact that one is fearful for their eternal safety may communicate itself. I believe this to be a legacy from the past, including the biblical past, from which Christianity must decisively withdraw itself, and for the following reasons: first, because we do *not* know about the eternal destiny of others and have therefore no right to be either fearful or hopeful; secondly, because an authentic sense of urgency in our witness towards all men can be based on the positive value to us of God's gifts of time and talents and on the intrinsic worth of the individual in God's sight. That is to say, there are other grounds than fear which can motivate the Christian gospel of the urgency of regarding each minute of our time as under God's judgement.

In this respect I think we may legitimately differentiate between some of the attitudes and actions attributed to Jesus by biblical writers, and attitudes and actions appropriate to ourselves. The writers of the gospels clearly believed that Jesus possessed divine insight into the hearts of those with whom he dealt. He knew what was passing in the minds of his

disciples (Luke 9.47); he could confidently assert that God saw
through the righteousness of the Pharisees (Luke 16.15); or,
as John explicitly testifies, 'he knew men so well, all of them,
that he needed no evidence from others about a man, for he
himself could tell what was in a man' (John 2.24–25, NEB).
Under such conditions the positive and immediate categorisa-
tion of the fate of the saved and of the lost which we find in
the gospels may be much more readily intelligible. The historical question of whether Jesus himself used hope of reward
and fear of punishment in his own teaching, difficult enough to
solve on purely historical grounds, needs to be related both to
the evangelist's convictions about Jesus and to our own
estimate of his power.

But it is another thing entirely for Christians to claim such
power, and for them to imitate Jesus in this respect may be
positively misleading. There is the danger, of which every
'pastor' |ought to be aware, of trying to assume the rôle of
the Good Shepherd; that is of identifying a lost sheep and of
allowing him to think that if he refuses that call to be saved
there is no salvation for him. Experience teaches two hard
lessons, however: first, that men and women profess Christianity for a bewildering variety of good and bad reasons, and
equally refuse to profess for good and bad reasons; and
secondly, that some of those who profess for a time later fall
away. No pattern reveals itself in the bewildering interplay of
emotion and reason which constitutes men's attitudes towards
Christ and towards the Church. No Christian could be
satisfied for long if he made conversion to professing Christian
faith the sole aim of his relations with others. To evangelise
must mean much more than to seek to elicit an explicit
acknowledgement of Christ.

Having said that one is aware of the opposite danger of
failing to face the contemporary world with the seriousness of
its choices. In Christian faith this is true not merely in the

large decisions which dominate politics today, but in the daily choices by which men create their personal futures, and which affect the quality of their relations with others. The appeal to the teacher in the second letter to Timothy to press the message home on all occasions, to remain calm and sane, and to do all the duties of one's calling (2 Tim. 4.1–4, NEB) is a forceful reminder of the impossibility of resting content with facile optimism. Even if one is not prepared to make judgements about the eternal destiny of individuals, one may quite legitimately visualise the truly dreadful consequences here and now for a society which neglects the quality of life lived in and through the Christian gospel. Refusal to use the methods of fear in the one case should not blind the Christian to the real urgency of witness that the content of the gospel places upon him.

(iii) *Truth and certainty.* This is probably the most important consideration in relation to the dialogue between religions. For if one religion believes itself to possess a finally true revelation of God, it would seem to follow that it possesses certainty on any matter within its range of interpretation in which there might be a dispute. Or, conversely, that if that religion is prepared to admit that there is room for dispute in such matters of interpretation, it can scarcely claim the status of being 'the truth'. If we take seriously the consequences of pluriformity in Christian theology, we appear to be in the latter situation; that is, we are in some difficulty in being able to claim of our doctrinal formulations that they are true.

How would the situation appear to one of the brothers in the parable of the ring? He would *know* that the ring had been given him by his father; he would *believe* that his father had given him the true ring, despite the fact that he would see that all the rings could not be true; and he would *hope* that in the end, after the long period of experiential testing prescribed by the judge, his own would be publicly and irrefutably seen to be, in fact, genuine. Thus his sense of certainty would be a compound of knowledge, belief and hope.

This story cannot, of course, be used without further ado to explicate the position of a Christian as he contemplates 'other religions'. The part played by the father in the story is, in particular, an unacceptably naïve analogue of the supposed activity and purpose of God in the manifold religions of mankind. But at the same time the story usefully illustrates how a sense of certainty may be compounded of a number of elements, among which may be direct personal experience, belief based on memory and corroborative evidence, and hope based on reliable promises.

It is important, nevertheless, to point to the distinction between certainty and a sense of certainty, or certitude. On one definition of 'certain' it is not certain that the Christian faith is true, if the criteria for certainty are those used for certainty about the existence of objects in the physical world. For obviously certainty about faith cannot be the same as certainty about sense experience. The 'certainty' claimed in the New Testament for belief is inner certitude, and the 'knowledge' is described in terms of 'indwelling'. The evidence for such certitude and such knowledge is compounded of many elements.

In the first place there is personal experience. The event of Jesus was personally experienced, seen and touched by eye-witnesses, whose testimony, it is claimed, is embodied in the narratives. Further there are visions of Christ seen for example by Stephen and by Paul, and there are clear references to mystical experiences of various kinds throughout the New Testament.

Secondly there is belief. In belief the memory of a past experience becomes vividly real, or such experiences of others are seen to fit with one's own experience, each receiving confirmation by subsequent corroborative evidence. The familiar process of 'growth' in Christian faith is the outcome of corroboration.

And thirdly there is hope, or trust. Throughout the New Testament assurance of salvation is always associated with hope and with persistence in the faith. This hope is based on the promise of God that death will be swallowed up in victory; a promise which it is not possible to experience as actual except by passing through it in due time.

The purpose of briefly recapitulating these elements of the compound nature of Christian certitude is to illustrate the fact that the quality of the certitude admits a variety of interpretations. In the first place the historical experience of the event of Jesus is open to more than one historical interpretation, for example, on the precise content of his teaching or on the impression which he made. Then secondly with respect to belief, the previous life-experience of the believer clearly determines in part the form in which the Christian faith will be received by him, and the nature of his subsequent corroborative experiences. And thirdly his hope or truth is fully based upon the quality of his belief, and thus open to the same variables.

To exhibit the variety of interpretation admissible in the experience of Christian certitude is to demonstrate the falsity of the idea that the Christian already has indubitably certain answers to all matters of dispute in religion. That the Christian faith has specific content and that that content may be defended as true does not require the corollary that the content of no other faiths need be considered. Quite the reverse. The Christian faith is so utterly committed to speaking the truth, that dispute in religion must be a matter for the most rigorous and sympathetic inquiry. An arrogant or judgemental attitude is out of the question.

But how, it may be asked, can one both believe one's own faith to be true and 'sympathetically' investigate the faith of others? I believe this to be possible, not only because of the variety of interpretation which the Christian faith permits, but also because of the nature of faith itself. 'Faith' is neither a constant and unvarying, nor a steadily growing or declining state of consciousness. Faith is more like a theme song or a series of related theme songs constantly reoccurring in the course of an opera; or, alternatively, like a main character or characters in a novel whose deeds furnish the main plot. There will be in either case substantial periods of time when other themes or characters are introduced, whose comings and goings provide variety and diversion. Similarly with faith. It is not a boringly uniform state of mind precluding experiment. For the mind is in any case incapable of such uniform concentration of attention. It is constantly experimenting with new ways of looking at things some of which may be markedly at variance with its characteristic point of view.

In this way thinking through an alternative to the faith one holds is a perfectly possible activity; and one, indeed, by which experience may be enriched. Of course to experiment in this way with another religious interpretation of life is to expose oneself to the possibility that one may be convinced by it. Indeed there may be very many Christians who live for a time a painfully diverse life between faith and doubt, but whose faith is ultimately enriched by the experience and whose usefulness to others is thereby greatly increased. And there are those whose wrestlings with alternative interpretations of life lead them away from Christian faith altogether.

But the risk, if it is counted as a risk, is unquestionably worth it. For it is only an arrogant narrowmindedness that could imagine that a single life-experience was a sufficient basis for an interpretation of God's activity in and love for all creation.

We have looked briefly at three aspects of the Christian's problem when he considers 'other religions'. We have not, however, looked at any religion other than Christianity, which is unquestionably the next step. Unhappily it is one beyond the competence of the present writer. But in this very fact there lies, I believe, an important warning. To understand a religion, and the kind of claims for truth which it makes, is no easy task. Even within the richly explored field of Christianity it is quite commonly said that the three years full-time study which students may be able to give it simply bring them to the foothills; and this is not to mention the gifts of insight and maturity which the understanding of Christian faith demands in practice. In theological study specialisation is inevitable, and it is unreasonable to demand of an academic that he be well equipped to speak outside his main field.

But as we increasingly realise the importance of under-standing religions other than Christianity, even as a means of further deepening our grasp upon Christian faith itself, we are presenting ourselves with a stupendous intellectual task. The task has two facets. First, is the obvious matter of acquir-ing reliable information about 'other religions'; information, that is, which not merely 'informs' but which leads to sym-pathetic understanding. Then, secondly, there is the business of understanding the Christian approach to a dialogue of religions. It is this second facet of the task which we have begun to consider here. We have restricted ourselves to showing how and why Christianity is receptive to 'other religions', in order that interest in them should not be left to those who have become disenchanted with the Christian faith, or should be thought to be inconsistent with fidelity to it.

But a warning is necessary. It is certainly true that hitherto for much of the West the term 'religious' has meant Christian. Eastern religions are still largely unknown even to Western intellectuals, whose habits of mind have been formatively influenced by Christianity. The current demand, particularly in the context of Religious Education, for information about the whole field of the religious life of man is a sharp reaction to this domination of the west by the Christian world picture. It would be foolish to decry the demand; but the dangers of superficiality are obvious. It is only by knowing one faith well that the structure of another faith begins to take on any depth of meaning. Without any experience of worship, or of the integration of faith and life, one can scarcely begin to make any sense out of any other religion, particularly one in which the habit of contemplation may have been developed further than in Christianity and play a more important rôle. Some considerable caution will be needed, and real educational research, if the Religious Education of the future (which must certainly contain more about faiths other than Christianity) is not to fall as disastrously short of its aims as the bible based Religious Education stemming from the 1944 Act. And it is to be hoped that the movement of mature scholarship which is just beginning to produce basic texts and monographs will yield fruit in the deepening and broadening of the Christian's understanding of his place in the religious history of mankind.

8
THE CHARACTER OF CHRIST

IT is proposed in this final chapter to try to make some account
of the essence of Christianity, which we defined loosely as the
character or spirit of Christ. It will be recalled that the context
in which the need for such a definition arose was the existence
and persistence of doctrinal disagreements between Christians.
It was said that it would be intolerable if there were no hope of
ever being able to distinguish between differing views, and my
suggestion was that the character or spirit of Christ was some
kind of norm for Christianity. It remains therefore to unpack
somewhat this ambiguous-sounding phrase.

A preliminary is to offer some justification for the use of the
term 'Christ' outside the historical context of the ministry of
Jesus. The New Testament usage of the term our Lord Jesus
Christ, sandwiching the name 'Jesus' between two evaluative
designations of him, will be perfectly familiar if not self-
explanatory. We need not suppose that it will be easy, or even
possible, to point to similar instances where the influence of an
historical individual is spoken of so personally as his living
presence. To speak of the 'living Christ' is to speak of his
influence; but still more, it is to speak of his presence, beyond
the natural category of influence, in mystical indwelling. The
language is no more obscure than language about the activity
of God in any instance where human co-activity is included.
If it is possible to speak of God 'being' in Christ, then we may
also speak of the spirit of Christ 'being' in men today. To use
the term 'spirit of Christ' rather than 'spirit of God' is simply

to draw attention to attributes historically manifest in the event of Jesus Christ.

The first thing that must be said about the character of Christ is that its starting-point is a matter of history, for which all the critical art of the historian is relevant, if not sufficient. Jesus was an individual person, and individual people are amenable to historical treatment if the sources on them are reliable enough. In the case of Jesus the historical starting-point for any inquiry is unquestionably what the early Church thought about him and the account which they presented. This account is not just a flat chronicle of his actions, not just a psychological study of his personality, and not just a theological interpretation of his significance; but it is a mixture of all of these and this fact presents the theologian with his problems.

This is not to deny the right of the historian, *qua* historian, to say of any given narrative in the gospels that the evidence considered in itself is not sufficient to decide whether an event did or did not occur as reported. Nor is the theologian's concern to offer his theological convictions as an excuse for refusing to consider the historical evidence in its own right. But we should want to differentiate carefully between the following sorts of cases:

(a) Reports of events not involving the miraculous, where there is no historical reason for doubting the veracity of the writer (e.g. reports of sayings consistent with everything known about Jesus).

(b) Reports of events involving the miraculous, where there is no other reason for doubting the facts than general doubt about miracles.

(c) Reports of events, whether miraculous, or not, where there is good reason to suppose that they did not occur other than general doubt about miracles.

With regard to (a) and (c) the theologian and the historian

would be in complete agreement, and in establishing into which category any given story fell one and the same historical methods would be employed. That is to say, the Christian theologian would fully accept the use of rigorous methods of historical inquiry to help with the classification of all his material. But the difficulties start in relation to the very large quantity of material which may well be in class (b). Here it has to be admitted that theological and historical reason may part company. *Qua* historian, one's verdict on a miracle story might be ambiguous or agnostic; *qua* theologian one sets the report in a frame of reference which lends the story a new significance. Thus the report is not merely that such and such happened on a particular day, but that the event was part of a continuing activity of God in the world; and God's activity may not be circumscribed by our own man-made limits of the possible.

In what follows we are speaking from the standpoint of the theological frame of reference. It will be assumed that the historical task of classifying material and weighing evidence is constantly being performed with integrity. But the theological task presses further to inquire whether and to what extent the New Testament frame of reference on the significance of Jesus is true. By 'true' one does not necessarily mean originating with Jesus himself; though if it were a fact that some interpretations originated with him and others again were denied by him this would be at the very least a relevant consideration. But to ask whether an interpretation of Jesus' significance is true is to engage with other Christian theologians (in this case the writers of the New Testament) in a discussion of a matter of all-consuming mutual interest. He is discussing in fact what led them to write about Jesus at all.

It is evident, therefore, that for this discussion to proceed, it must begin with some kind of understanding of what the New Testament writers themselves say. That is not to imply that we must confine ourselves to understanding what they say; on the contrary we have the freedom and the right to ask questions which they did not ask and to offer new interpretations of which they could not have thought. (This is especially the case in the light of new knowledge about man since Darwin and Freud.) But the point remains that unless our questions and suggestions refer to and spring out of aspects of what these writers say, the discussion cannot any longer refer to Jesus, the historical figure, but to some imaginary being whom we are creating for our own purposes. To be able to begin to develop a view of the character or spirit of Christ we are bound to begin with, and constantly refer back to the New Testament witness to him and the historical studies to which it has given rise.

Concerning Jesus I propose to restrict myself to saying four things:

(a) that he had a special conception of his own vocation, and that this conception was expanded and developed in various ways after his resurrection;

(b) that, as a result of his sense of vocation, he strongly desired to help the sick and others in various kinds of bondage, and that after the resurrection his own death was interpreted as a great act of salvation;

(c) that he spoke prophetically about a kingdom or dominion of God in the context of which men would be able to serve God utterly, and that after his resurrection this dominion was understood to be partly a present reality and partly a hoped for event after the last judgement;

(d) that he called men into discipleship to himself, and that after the resurrection this call was gradually developed into a sense of a community living in the closest relationship to God through the Spirit.

These four are undeniably among the most important items of the New Testament witness to Jesus; also undeniable is the fact that there are other topics and that the above four are a selection. The ministry of Jesus does not readily lend itself to schematisation, and there are drawbacks in doing so. But in the present scheme there is a particular purpose which must now be explained.

It is proposed to elucidate the character of Christ under four heads, but as a whole. The four heads are those indicated as based in the ministry of Jesus, but the 'wholeness' of Christ demands that they should not be presented in a flat series. By 'wholeness' I mean to indicate that the ministry of Christ and the Christian religion which springs from it, is a phenomenon which engages the whole being of a man. To be a Christian means not merely to believe certain things but also to engage in certain forms of worship or to express certain attitudes in prayer and to guide one's activities in certain sorts of ways. It is a many-sided profession in which the various aspects interlock and interrelate. One of the chief results of having studied the history of Christian life and belief as expressed over the centuries is to realise how even slight adjustments to the balance of aspects in Christianity give rise to great shifts of emphasis, movements and even schism in the Christian com- munity. To do justice to Christianity as a phenomenon it is necessary to make some attempt to preserve its wholeness; and a preliminary to that is to attempt to specify the diverse elements of Christian life.

Three aspects have been chosen here, corresponding to an ancient tripartite division of human character into intellect, emotion and will.

(a) Christian life unquestionably involves assent to the truth of certain doctrines. It may be the case that any particular proposition may not express the final truth of any given doctrine; but it cannot be denied that there is intellectual content in Christianity, and that intellectual effort of some order (even of the most elementary sort) has to be expended in order to grasp it.

(b) In relation to emotion there is more difficulty. What is undeniable is that the practice of prayer and worship has characterised Christianity from the first. It is also clear that prayer is not primarily an intellectual activity. Whether we designate all that religious experience which the life of prayer entails as an 'emotional' involvement is perhaps less clear. But there exists a dimension of Christian life in worship and prayer which needs to be given full weight in any attempt to present its wholeness.

(c) Finally, Christianity entails a whole series of consequences for personal moral activity and the ordering of social life, springing from the determination of the will. Christianity is inescapably a faith with a pronounced moral character, to which justice must always be done.

We have, therefore, at least these three aspects to consider in order to embrace some part of the many-sidedness of Christian life.

Here, too, one is bound to add that schematisation tends to hide the very closeness with which these aspects relate to each other in practice. It is noticeable, for example, that in one strand at least of the New Testament each one of these aspects is brought under the guidance of God's Spirit; so that understanding is a gift of the Spirit, prayer is through the Spirit and the Christian virtues are the fruit of the Spirit. As the whole life of man is brought under the Spirit's influence, the signs of the consistency and interrelatedness of his guidance are the more clear.

We have in the two preceding sections established a scheme for the interpretation of the character of Christ as follows:

The Ministry of Jesus as 1 Vocation
2 Salvation

3 Dominion
4 Relationship

The Christian life as (a) Doctrine
(b) Prayer
(c) Action

It remains for us to interpret each of the four cited aspects of the ministry of Jesus in terms of the three cited aspects of Christian life.

1(a) *Vocation—doctrine.* We begin rightly with Christology, the doctrine of the person of Christ. The term 'vocation' tends to emphasise the role which he saw himself fulfilling, and is in some respects unsatisfactory. The proper subject matter of the doctrine of the person of Christ is his essential being, to which his role or function is indeed relevant but secondary. But the important question which theology has raised with particular acuteness in the last 200 years is the way in which and the extent to which an account of that essential being of Christ may be laid out in propositional form and be made amenable to intellectual understanding. In this period it has been both helped and hampered by historical speculations about how Jesus himself may have interpreted his own vocation; for whereas in earlier centuries theologians had been prepared to accept all the gospel evidence, critical research sometimes radically reconstructed it. In some of these reconstructions Jesus' own consciousness of being in a special sense 'sent from God' is seriously reduced or denied, with consequential difficulties for traditional Christology. Also changes in attitude towards metaphysics have influenced the extent to which some theologians have been prepared to try and specify anything about the essential being of God. The last 200 years have accordingly been a period of most intense activity in Christological interpretation.

I

The task of Christology, however, is one and the same, namely, to bring the person of Christ into relation with the activity of God. It is here that the influence of naturalistic interpretations of the significance of Jesus needs to be observed. By 'naturalistic' I mean an interpretation which does not pass beyond natural categories, for example, those of teacher, martyr for conscience or morally admirable leader. Particularly since the start of the nineteenth century the 'life of Jesus' has exercised a considerable fascination for many writers, who have developed or sponsored portraits of Jesus as a human figure sympathetic to their own times. Strauss's *Life of Jesus* (1835/6) has already been mentioned; another example is the book of the same name by the Frenchman, J. E. Renan (1823–92), published in 1863. More recent portraits have concentrated on some of the revolutionary traits of Jesus in the gospels. Attractive though these may have been, or be, the theologian's task in Christology is bound to make him suspicious not merely of the results of such attempts, but of the methods and more particularly the assumptions underlying them. To portray a natural Jesus of whom for some, usually unexplained, reason it is possible to speak of in connection with speaking of God is not a satisfactory Christology. The event of Jesus itself must be sufficient to suggest and to bear the weight of the appropriateness of relating him to the activity of God. Even if the interpretative model is no more than Spirit-inspired prophethood (a category which the New Testament documents explicitly regard as less than satisfactory), there must be corresponding activity in the ministry of Jesus to which to point in corroboration. And if the categories are to be as rich in suggestiveness as Son of God or Divine Word (logos), then similarly the ministry and life of Jesus must evidence their appropriateness. The possibilities in Christological interpretation are clearly many, and the principal of pluriformity in doctrine unquestionably applies. But in as much as it may be itself a matter of doctrinal dispute, Christology has to be held to the norm of the character of Christ as that character is evident in all its many other aspects.

1(b) *Vocation—prayer.* There are three characteristic attitudes which New Testament Christology immediately suggest. The first, from the Synoptic Gospels and Paul, is the use of the intimate term 'Abba' in address to God. The opening word of the prayer taught by Christ to his disciples, it expresses a peculiarly personal and close relationship with God. Secondly, entirely consistent with this, is the theme of the dependence of Jesus upon God, and of Jesus' disciples upon him, taught with great explicitness and wealth of elaboration in the Fourth Gospel. The third attitude is that of humility, said in several passages in Paul to be the attitude of Christ himself in his incarnation.

The fact of Christology, the relating of the person of Christ to the activity of God, has the effect of commending what is said to be Christ's attitude to God to those who seek to be his followers. This is expressed in prayer in the sense of child-like, though not childish, dependence upon God, trust in his providence and submission to his will.

1(c) *Vocation—action.* In the New Testament one very important, eventually realised effect of Christology was the breaking down for Jesus' Jewish disciples of the age-long separation from Samaritans and Gentiles. The realisation of the common brotherhood of men in the sight of God, though long delayed in its full practical expression, was a very early spiritual realisation of Christianity, as references to slavery in the letters to Paul show. There are several strands in this idea of brotherhood. One is the unification of humanity in the humanity of Christ; for to be human was to be on a par with all other humans, whose humanity gives them, too, a natural relationship to Christ. A second strand consequent on this is

the affirmation of human dignity and worth; because Christ
acts on behalf of all men, all share the common worth of 'those
for whom Christ died'. Here again the practical expression in
social and political order has emerged only a long time after
the implantation of the idea at a personal or spiritual level.
Our increased knowledge about the effect on the human spirit
of grinding poverty or political impotence has contributed
greatly to our sense of urgency about righting injustices. This
is an instructive illustration of the way in which the initial
Christian revolution in attitude towards the worth of the
individual has, with the help of psychology and the social
sciences, had remarkable repercussions in contemporary
social and political attitudes.

The characteristics (1a, b and c) which we have mentioned
spring from the historical fact that Jesus was who he was and
had the impact which he had. This is not at all to deny that in
each case historical puzzles exist which may affect the precise
way in which any one of the elements may be developed. But
it is my contention that if the wholeness of the character of
Christ is to be glimpsed then the three must be interrelated.
Christological doctrine cannot be developed out of the context
of worship or of ethical action without distortion to the character of Christ, which has in each of these areas the specific
traits mentioned.

2(a) *Salvation—doctrine.* The technical term in theology for
salvation-doctrine is soteriology, and one of the traditional
concerns of this section is the development of a theory of
atonement. This attempts to describe the whole working of the
plan of salvation as God's response to the misery of the human
situation. But our method requires that we take our point of
departure from the ministry of Jesus in which the type of total
theory eventually produced in atonement doctrine is not much
evident. Indeed if one were to confine oneself to the Synoptic

Gospels it would be difficult to develop such a theory at all. For these theories tend to concentrate upon the meaning of the death of Christ, upon which there is in the Synoptic Gospels, comparatively speaking, little interpretative reflection.

At the same time it is unquestionable from the gospel records that Jesus possessed and exercised power over many forms of sickness, especially demon possession, and that he did so because he was moved with compassion for the sufferers. Whether it is possible to link this compassionate ministry to the sick both with his teaching and with his suffering and death remains one of the principal historical puzzles of the New Testament. The evangelists record that Jesus both expected to be killed and interpreted his coming death as an act of service for others (Mark 10.45 and parallels), an offering (like a sacrifice) which confirmed or established a covenant between God and man (Mark 14.24). Some historians of the New Testament have questioned whether Jesus himself ever in fact gave such interpretations, which admittedly occupy a small part of the Synoptic Gospels. It is probably not possible for us to do more than guess at the answer, which remains a matter of history. What is not to be doubted, however, is that after his resurrection the whole work of Christ came increasingly to be seen as turning upon the significance of his death. In John's Gospel, Jesus is the Saviour of the world, whose death was a banishment of the present evil Prince of the world and a sign by which all men would be drawn to himself (John 12.30–33). So also, and still more explicitly, for Paul Jesus' death was an expiatory sacrifice liberating men from bondage to sin (Rom. 3.23–25). Not unnaturally Jesus' healing of specific diseases or his freeing specific individuals suffering from demon possession falls into the background as the liberating effect of his ministry is felt to extend beyond the actual scenes of his activity. Among the links between the two are the word to save (s~zein, Gk), which is used both of healing and of spiritual salvation, and the frequency with which faith in the healer is said to be a precondition of both sorts of 'salvation'.

Like Christology, soteriology has been substantially affected in the last 200 years by historical study and by changes in philosophy. Naturalism has also been influential in support of theories restricting the effect of the work of Christ to the inspirational power of his 'heroic' self-sacrifice. But as in the case of Christology, soteriology only begins when someone is prepared to make some statements relating the work of Christ to the plan and purpose of God. The New Testament consistently does so in relation to God's loving purposes for mankind and his rejection and condemnation of sin. But the variety of possible constructions within this broad area is, if anything, still greater than in Christology, with which it is intimately linked. In comparison with Christology, soteriology has never received the high degree of precise formulation evident in the definitions of the fifth-century ecumenical councils. Soteriology is furthermore, very responsive to the variety of descriptions of the human situation offered in the history of theology and in philosophical anthropology to the present. Indeed it is questionable whether the variety of human conditions and sorts of bondage lends itself to the generalised treatment accorded them in most traditional theories of the atonement. The preservation of variety may well be one of the most important tasks of contemporary soteriology.*

2(b) *Salvation—prayer.* In traditional doctrines of the atonement Christ's suffering and death, which was for us (*pro nobis*), was also in some sense caused by our sins. Thus a collect might speak of our abounding in 'sorrow for our sins

* See particularly, F. W. Dillistone, *The Christian Understanding of the Atonement* (London, 1968).

which were the cause of thy passion'.* Popularised modern psychology has denigrated what it calls 'guilt feelings' as something unhelpful and unhealthy if no actual justification for them exists. And where no credence is given to the idea that 'sin' is a genuinely objective reality, the sense of sin which has frequently accompanied profession of Christian faith has been singled out for special condemnation. Unquestionably modern psychology has offered new models of the structure and development of the moral sense or conscience, and has tended to relativise such sense to the early relationships of mother and infant.† Penitence or sorrow for sin can frequently be the name given to states of anxiety which has an almost wholly explicable background in these early relationships.

There are, however, many indications in traditional spirituality of awareness of the danger of bogus guilt feelings. 'For godly grief produces a repentance that leads to salvation and brings no regret, but worldly grief produces death' (2 Cor. 7.10 (RSV)). Paul's use of the word 'godly' emphasises the fact that to be real, sorrow for one's sin has to be sorrow for falling short of that which God himself has shown in Jesus to be the goal of human life, namely fellowship with God. That the concept of God has psychologically derived meaning for everyone is not deniable. But the Christian position is that this psychologically derived meaning must be criticised and corrected by reference to Jesus and his demands.

When the Christian, therefore, confesses and feels sorry for his sin—an abiding element in Christian prayer—he is not simply re-enacting the infantile struggle for a satisfactory relationship with his mother; he is comparing his own behaviour with some specific goals which he has been taught by Christ to desire and to long for; and these are goals which others may well *not* long for, indeed may explicitly reject.

* A collect in the office of Compline.
† e.g. R. S. Lee, *Your Growing Child and Religion* (Harmondsworth).

There is therefore an important element of objectivity about the sense of sorrow for sin which characterises Christian prayer.

2(c) *Salvation—action.* It is the Lord's Prayer itself which makes clear the ethical aspect of soteriology: 'Forgive us the wrong we have done, as we have forgiven those who have wronged us' (Matt. 6.12, Luke 11.4). The duty of forgiveness is one of the most striking characteristics of the Christian life, and is taught clearly in a number of Jesus' parables. Its basis and source in Christianity is the awareness which the individual has of his own state of wrong relationship with God and of his meeting forgiving grace in response to his petition. This fact makes clear the difference between forgiveness and toleration, with which it is frequently confused in the modern mind. God's forgiveness of sin is not an urbane toleration of it. In this sense Christianity may be rightly accused of intolerance; indeed it may be that in its history it has too frequently tolerated offences to the individual and his worth and dignity. For it is one thing to turn the other cheek when one is unjustly struck oneself; it is quite another to tolerate indignity committed against the persons of others.

The duty of forgiveness cannot and does not stand in isolation from other aspects of the character of Christ. Abstraction of a characteristic from its whole setting leads to absurd conclusions in social and political life particularly when one asks about the relevance of forgiveness to personal ambition, national sovereignty or self-defence. It is not that forgiveness is out of the question in relation to public or international affairs, but that other considerations from Christian theology also apply in relation to the goals of human life. For forgiveness has always, as in soteriology had as its aim the restoration of broken relationships in accordance with specific goals of living. The important thing is that forgiveness of an acknowledged wrong should be retained, contrary to the natural retaliatory inclination of wronged individuals and groups, as a possible course of action in pursuit of the desired reconciliation.

3(a) *Dominion—doctrine.* There are two natural foci of the doctrine of God's reign in the New Testament, Jesus' preaching of the kingdom of God and his resurrection and ascension. As in the case of soteriology it is not immediately clear that the two are intimately linked in Jesus' own ministry. Certainly entering the kingdom of God, winning eternal life and being saved are, as far as the evangelists are concerned, identical (Mark 10.17–31), but they are not brought into close relationship with Jesus' own expectation of being raised from the dead by the power of God. Here again it seems that the resurrection introduces a new perspective, fruitfully explored initially by Paul, but also by the author of the Fourth Gospel. Christ's resurrection becomes central to the interpretation of Christian life. For Paul it is the same power as that which brought Christ from the dead which gives new life to the Christian (Rom. 8.9–11). And for John, it is through faith in the risen Lord that a man comes to possess eternal life himself (John 11.21–27, 20.26–31). The theme of conquest by God's power links the teaching of Jesus about the kingdom with the interpretation of Christ's resurrection, much in the way that that of liberation links the two elements of soteriology.

Here again historical study in the last 200 years of Christian theology has had a profound effect on the way the doctrine has been developed. On the one hand a considerable effort has been made to grasp the meaning of 'the kingdom of God' in the teaching of Jesus, involving sometimes radical reconstructions of the witness of the gospels; and, on the other hand, the resurrection stories have continued to attract critical attention. Once again it cannot be said that the historians have been able to present us with many 'assured results'. Indeed in relation to the resurrection the problem is exceedingly acute; for only someone with special reasons for taking the gospel testimony seriously would bother with a narrative of a physical resurrection written forty or more years after the event.* That Paul does not describe such a resurrection may, indeed, count somewhat against the purely historical evidence for it. But I repeat that except for special reason, no one would ordinarily pause to consider such a story, or to suppose that Paul was doing anything other than grossly misusing language when he spoke of Christ as being 'raised to life' on the grounds of a few appearances to disciples, including himself.† If anything other than a purely naturalistic account is to be given of these assertions, then the differences between one theological interpretation and another, though real, will not seem as great as they perhaps do to some theologians.

Thus, as with Christology and soteriology, theological interpretation only begins when the stories of the resurrection and ascension of Christ are related to the whole nature of God's dominion over the world. The interrelation of the subject matter of Christian doctrine becomes at once apparent in the fact that the nature of our hope both of victory over sin and evil and of the surmounting of death turn upon the account given of Christ's resurrection and ascension.

3(b) *Dominion—prayer*. The attribution of victorious power to God is one of the major themes of Christian prayer. Indeed in the letter to the Hebrews, the writer closely connects the ascension of Christ with the Christian's right of access to God. Prayer 'through Jesus Christ, our Lord' is prayer which claims the whole victorious work of Christ as the ground of being heard by God and is thus confident of his mercy and grace.

* By 'physical', I mean one which involves the physical removal of Christ's body from the tomb by a force other than body-snatchers.
† See 1 Cor. 15.

The joyful confidence of the Christian in all the changing circumstances of life was from the start a pronounced characteristic. In adversity it was able to give grounds for and to sustain hope, and in favourable times to prevent pride and self-satisfaction. Joy in God, which is a feature of the mystical writing of more than one religion, is thus given an objective focus in the ministry and resurrection of Christ. The not infrequent experiences of spiritual torment or dryness are a pathway through the dark night of spiritual death to the dawn of a new resurrection. The images of light and life, so powerful in the religious life of man, are given concrete reality as uncertainty about the future or anxiety about death can be related to the Easter event.

3(c) *Dominion—action.* In the realm of ethics the dominion of God is most powerfully seen in the effect of the specific hope of Christians upon their interpretation of human destiny. This has admittedly been subject to considerable shifts of emphasis in the last 200 years, as specific mundane hopes have been strongly emphasised or re-emphasised alongside and sometimes in place of hopes of heaven. It was the philosopher Kant (1724–1804) who at the end of the eighteenth century in his work on religion strongly emphasised 'the kingdom of God' as a hoped-for goal of human endeavour. His work began the ending of Christian passivity in the face of the evils of this present world, and indirectly led, among other effects, to the Communism of Karl Marx (1818–83).

It is in relation to the goals of human society that most of the recent phenomenal achievements of science and technology pose problems; and because they are problems never posed before in the same way, strenuous efforts of ethical thought have to be given to them. It is clear, however, that we cannot presume on agreement between men on the purposes of life, or indeed even on the supposition that life has a purpose or purposes. It remains ambiguous what qualities of living are going to be promoted by the inescapable decisions which confront us. The Christian can help here by making concrete in his own life's standards and quality the character of Christ. By continually putting first God's kingdom and righteousness he may be able to provide for a whole society its unconscious assumptions and goals.

4(a) *Relationship—doctrine*. It is clear that, if the traditional structure of Christian theology is to be preserved at all, at this point it becomes necessary to speak of the Holy Spirit; but the title of the present section is relationship. The difficulty of deriving a doctrine of the Holy Spirit from the New Testament is notorious, and was noticed and acknowledged at the very time that the divinity of the Holy Spirit as a third person in the Trinity was being defined.* Yet what needs to be said in this section concerns the whole mode of the life of God with men, for which the term 'Spirit' is both scriptural and suggestive. In the Synoptic Gospels it is the Spirit who comes upon Mary causing her to conceive and who descends upon Jesus at his baptism in the form of a dove. In Acts it is the Spirit who directs the expansion of the Christian Church, and, in the Fourth Gospel, who is to abide with the disciples for ever teaching and guiding them into the truth. Differences of conception and presentation notwithstanding, the mode of God's presence with men is spiritual since God is Spirit.

The call to discipleship is a call into a new relationship with God, characterised by faith in Christ. In the Synoptic Gospels, where the activities and teaching of Jesus himself holds the centre of the stage, the spiritual nature of discipleship is rarely considered, though an uncharacteristic passage speaks

* Gregory of Nazianzus (329–89), among the earliest of the Fathers to formulate what later became orthodox Trinitarian theology, spoke of the revelation of the Holy Spirit as being adumbrated in the New Testament, but only made clear in the later Church.

of 'knowing the Father' through the Son (Matt. 11.25–27, Luke 10.21–22). In the Fourth Gospel, and above all in Paul's letters, the nature of Christian discipleship now that Jesus himself has withdrawn his physical presence is the subject of considerable theological reflection. The two writers unhesitatingly turn to the doctrine of the Spirit. For the writer of the Fourth Gospel, the Spirit of truth will maintain and preserve the witness of the disciples to Jesus.* For Paul, the Spirit of God (or of Christ—the terms are interchangeable) simply *is* the life of the Christian disciple.† For both Paul and the writer of the first letters of John (whether identical with the writer of the Fourth Gospel or not) discipleship is alternatively described as dwelling in Christ, dwelling in God and possessing God's Spirit.

Precisely this looseness of language led to the orthodox doctrine of the Trinity, as three co-equal persons in one undivided Godhead, and to the ambitious attempts at providing analogies to assist the understanding. In one of the most impressive of these attempts, Augustine of Hippo (354–430) speaks of the Spirit as the life principle of God, or as the love of Father for Son and of Son for Father. The appropriateness for Augustine of making love the particular characteristic of the spirit derives from the conjunction of the biblical statements that God is spirit (John 4.24) and that God is love (1 John 4.16). But a further and more compelling reason lies in the Christian understanding of relationship. Consistently throughout the New Testament, from the two great commandments enunciated by Jesus to the great hymn in 1 Cor. 13, love is exalted as the bond of the relationship of God with men, and of men with each other. If the life of God itself is to be spoken of at all in terms of relationship, then there is no other alternative to describing that life as one of mutual love.

At the same time, the doctrine of the Trinity has been sub-

* See John 14–16. † See Rom. 8.

jected to considerable criticism in the last 200 years particularly from those who object to its over-confident, yet speculative, appearance. If the attempt is not to be made of offering analogies by which to understand the life of God in itself, then it is possible that a less ambitious way may be sought in describing the *effect* of the self-revelation of God, as Father, Son and Holy Spirit. In this case, love is the mode of operation of God upon the world—'God loved the world so much that he gave his only Son' (John 3.16 (NEB)). Here again there is more than one possibility of which the principle of pluriformity in doctrine can profitably take note.

4(b) *Relationship—prayer.* The whole mystical side of Christianity grows naturally out of the language of indwelling, being and abiding in Christ, used in Johannine and Pauline writing. It is by this indwelling that the Christian seeks the fulfilment of the will of God in himself; this is the focus of his identity and aspiration in the world; this is the principle of his wholeness and vitality. It is this that makes his prayer not merely an individual act, but the taking up of the individual with his joys and sorrows, his praises and his petitions into the will of God being fulfilled on earth, as it is in heaven.

This too is what is designated 'loving God'—the sum of the creature's response to his creator and the reflection of the creator's own gift. It is important that love towards God be allowed to have meaning and content outside the consequential love of man for man. The distinguishing of the two has been a point of particular difficulty in recent theology, which has greatly emphasised their interrelatedness. Albrecht Ritschl (1822–89), an influential liberal theologian, commented that love of God has no sphere outside love of one's neighbour.* But the unquestionable fact of the interrelatedness of the

* A. T. Swing, *The Theology of Albrecht Ritschl* (New York, 1901), p. 175. The work includes a translation of Ritschl's *Unterricht in der christliche Religion* (1875).

themes of Christian theology need not mean that they should be equated in content. In relation to the theme of love towards God there are some important pastoral implications of this latter assertion; as, for example, where two people loving each other are aware of God as a common reference point, by which the quality of their love for each other is constantly reshaped and enriched.

4(c) *Relationship—action.* Under this heading it is necessary first to speak of personal relationships with 'brethren', by which the New Testament means fellow Christians. Brotherly love is not general kindliness, but rather the calibre of relationships within the body of Christ. It should be noted that kindliness may be a good deal less demanding than love of the brethren. In the latter case love runs many more risks, as the not infrequent outbreak of unforgiving bitterness in Christian circles shows. If one has given of oneself in love, one is deeply vulnerable. When Peter asks how often he is to forgive a brother who keeps on wronging him, Jesus' reply is that forgiveness must have no end (Matt. 18.21–22); on no other condition is love of the brethren possible. The Church is thus the community of mutual love and forgiveness, constituting in itself the body of Christ and the initial environment of the Christian's ethical activity.

This apparently narrow preoccupation of parts of the New Testament with relationships within the Christian community has one important function when we consider the quality of the individual's relationships beyond confessional boundaries. It is perfectly realistic to consider that no notice is likely to be taken of one who preaches love, but who practises intrigue and bitterness in his own family. To be a Christian involves being able to point concretely to the love of God at work in the hearts of men; and one of the lessons for the Churches to learn is how to conduct their disagreements with frankness, yet without mistrust and envy. With the subject of love we are constantly liable to self-deception. If ever there was a traditional doctrine in need of critical examination, that is the doctrine of the Church as the body of Christ. If the Christian had only the Churches to point to as evidence of the character of Christ, his message would be fatally handicapped. Can it be accidental that Jesus' prime illustration of love of the neighbour concerned not a straightforward issue among co-religionists, nor even a Jew–Gentile encounter, but one between Jew and Samaritan, a co-existing and yet rival believer from the same basic family?

It is then only on the basis of relationships already established that the Christian can offer his love to the wider world as a socially cohesive virtue. Here he has to think both individually and as a member of his various social groups; this love in which he is rooted has to overflow into all his personal relationships, and wider still into the character of society. Love comes to assume so many diverse forms that if it has no common basis it would hardly be recognisable as the same virtue. What would courtesy towards one's colleagues have in common with a political decision about tax or law reform, for example? It would only be related if the individual could see it as arising out of a common source of inspiration.

One aspect of social behaviour deserves special mention at this time, namely the extent to which moral activity is determined by the structure of society. The study of sociology has offered some extremely important insights into the way in which society defines for us our freedom to act as moral beings. The importance of sociology for Christian ethics has not yet perhaps been fully grasped, even though it has been clear for long enough how closely involved Churches are in the social order of their societies. Examples in our own times in Germany, South Africa and Rhodesia have shown how important it is for a Church to be capable, if necessary, of opposing the social policies of a government. The depth of a Church's commitment to any one dominant social order needs to be kept under constant review, if its freedom to express the love of God in the complexities of a society is not to be lost.

Such then is the outline of the content of the phrase, the character of Christ. It is now possible to recognise more fully the appropriateness of the term 'character'. For a character to be real, it has to have the quality of depth and of wholeness. We may confidently claim as a well-based historical judgement that whatever else Jesus himself may have been, he was a many-sided and complex individual. If it is the Christian's business to reproduce that character, or rather such aspects of it as he is, by God's grace, able to reproduce, then he is bound to be guided by some conception of it *in its wholeness*. Just as the proper appreciation of a man's character involves exposure to its many facets, so with Christianity unless one has come to some understanding of it in its many-sidedness, it will be fatally easy to make oversimplified or unbalanced statements about it.

It remains, finally, to make some suggestions about how such a conception of the character of Christ can function as a norm in Christian theology by acting as a guide in the event of doctrinal disagreement.

In the first place, the character of Christ is a whole. Any attempt to describe it, although it may be organised as above to insure that as many aspects of it are covered as possible, must nevertheless ultimately stand or fall, as any character description, by its lifelike wholeness. Theology has been in the recent past a too onesidedly intellectualised discipline, insufficiently aware of the interrelation between doctrine, worship and ethics. If the task of the Christian is to be part of the contemporary expression of the character of Christ, the

K

task of the Christian theologian is to visualise the wholeness of that character.

Thus it is a perfectly correct procedure in the context of doctrinal disagreement to argue from the standpoint of the wholeness of the character of Christ. A position could not be defended if it was simply inconsistent with a characteristic of another kind in the total structure (a doctrine, for example, which lead to consequences contradicting the morality of Christianity or a devotional practice incapable of assimilation into the content of doctrine). This sort of internal inconsistency can also arise when a novel doctrinal interpretation necessitates an almost total overhaul of traditional devotion and morality. It is noteworthy, in this respect, that the 'new theology' and the 'new morality' have not produced anything remotely like a 'new devotion'.

Wholeness is one thing, systematisation is another. It would be possible to produce a systematic presentation of the Christian faith, which though thoroughly internally consistent was nevertheless a gross distortion of it. Systematisation can only be based on an enunciated principle of order; but character description does not lead itself to this sort of tidiness. It has been proved on countless occasions that to make one feature of a character the central interpretative key results in distortion. So, I believe, with interpreting the character of Christ. It is not systematisation which is required but a method whereby each characteristic is expounded by reference to each other. Thus in terms of the presentation of this chapter, a better exposition than successively reviewing 1 (a) (b) (c) (d), 2 (a) (b) (c) (d) and so forth would have been to expound 1 (a), not merely in the light of 1 (b), 1 (c) and 1 (d), but also in the light of 2 (a), 2 (b), 2 (c) and 2 (d) and so forth. It is something like this method of procedure which Karl Barth followed in his unfinished *Church Dogmatics* and which is responsible for its great length!

There is a second way in which the character of Christ may function as a norm. This concerns the experiential testing which theological concepts receive when lived out in Christian witness in the world. The appeal to experience is frequent in the New Testament, which clearly knew the situation of pluriformity at close quarters. The presence of spurious Christianity was to be detected in practical, as well as theoretical, ways. Those who did evil things were not to be received as teachers (Matt. 7.15–20; Luke 6.43–45).

This teaching has the important function of drawing attention to the interrelatedness of teaching and living in Christianity. And many other places in the New Testament go further and affirm the hollowness of making apparently correct doctrinal statements where the practice is contradictory. This is familiar enough. But there is a reverse influence to consider, namely, the effect that a certain environment may have on the way the Christian believes.

We are not now considering the unquestionable thesis of the sociology of religion that society is, at the least, one of a number of factors which condition the form which a given belief takes. I am referring here to the further fact that, in attempting to practise his faith, the Christian lives in an ambiguous environment which partly accepts and partly rejects what he stands for. By living experience he may come in due time to recognise what aspects of the faith as delivered to him help him in resisting evil and in doing good. In this way he has a constant check on the relevance to his actual experience of the teaching which he derives from the Christian Church. Slowly it may become clear that certain ways of formulating Christian doctrine do not meet what is needed in a given situation, whereas others do.

This kind of appeal to experience is, however, difficult to control. Like the appeal to the guidance of the Holy Spirit, it may be used in a mistaken manner as justification for views already embraced on other grounds. Furthermore it may not provide a universally valid criterion, since experience is so diverse. Thus the theology which seems relevant and valid in one man's situation, may equally well seem irrelevant in another's. The helpfulness or otherwise of a doctrine is not the same thing as its truth.

However, the appeal to experience is not simply a matter of whether this or that doctrine appears relevant or works out in practice. It is also a question of maintaining in a manner perceptible to the whole of mankind the living breadth of the character of Christ. For each individual Christian whether theologian or not, this is a task far beyond the confines of his own abilities and limitations. This is a matter of whether human life as a whole in our day and age bears the stamp of the character of Christ; for this result the inadequacy and partiality of our own individual contribution is only too evident. The Christian may try to express the character of Christ in his life; as a theologian he may do so in his thought. But whether this thought measures up to the character of Christ may to some extent be judged by what God is *himself* doing in the world.

The responsibility of Christian theology is not simply a matter of conveying a tradition of thought from one generation to another according to its own rules of internal development. That much will be apparent to all who are concerned to see the Christian Church as an active force in the modern world. Thus the question is not whether theology can be 'modernised' or 'brought up to date'; the real question is whether theology is or is not about the world which is developing around us. It is not a question of 'christianizing' the advances in medical science, biochemical research or industrial technology; they are so closely a matter of man's own future that they themselves are among the criteria for a valid theology.

This sort of appeal to experience, which insists on the activity of God *outside* the Church as much as it does within it, is always open to the charge of being facilely optimistic about human progress. But we are not dealing here with a naïve optimism about the future of humanity. The Judaeo-Christian concept of God has always combined the activity of God and the responsibility of man in forceful tension. To be taken into the promised land imposed far-reaching duties, and failure to perform them resulted in near catastrophe. For us the promised land is the extension of human dominion over nature, which began with man's first acts of tool-making. To be delivered from subservience to external circumstances into a more creative freedom is itself a partial fulfilment of God's will for man as understood by Christian faith. As long as theology seeks to give an account of divine activity, this deliverence from human bondage must be part of the whole picture of the character of Christ present in the world today.

For the Christian to enter fully into these new freedoms requires a special effort, since so much of the past has been dominated by passivity and acceptance. Not that a wholesale overthrow of the theology of the Christian centuries is required nor is acceptance an 'outmoded' concept. Rather, it is the case that the validity of Christian theology in the modern world is rightly judged by its ability to live creatively in the new freedoms. To deny that we ought to know certain things which might give a large measure of control over the future of the human race is a failure of nerve. The means whereby we acquire such knowledge and our consequential use of it, however, raise all the problems of the nature of humanity for which the Christian faith ought to be uniquely equipped to deal; hence an important experiential check on any new doctrinal interpretations of Christianity will be whether they make possible a firm handling of such problems. Any failure in this direction would be a failure to measure up to the character of Christ present among us today.

It will be apparent that these appeals to experience cannot

themselves be operated by the mere intellectual activity of the theologian. His job is done when he has offered a way of viewing Christian faith in the contemporary world. What remains, apart from his own attempt faithfully to express his convictions in his own life's context, is careful observation of the consequences of the theological activity of his generation in the life of the world around him. Only in this way can theology preserve the vitality and vigour of its own intellectual activity, the necessary reference to the personal activity of living the Christian faith, and the co-operative response of non-theologians, Christian or not, to its attempts to interpret and to depict the character of Christ.

BIBLIOGRAPHY

THE following bibliography is designed to suggest further reading of various sorts relevant to the material covered in each chapter.

1 – Liberalism in Theology

A review of the way the Bible has been used in the Church throughout its history may be found in R. M. Grant, *A Short History of the Interpretation of the Bible* (London, 1965). For the impact of science on religion, see A. Richardson, *The Bible in the Age of Science* (London, 1961).* The Victorian controversies about science, doubt and the Bible are delightfully told in W. O. Chadwick, *The Victorian Church*, Vol. II (London, 1970), Chapters i–iii. It is a mistake to think that there is an agreed scientific view of man, so long as scientists disagree so widely about man's moral and/or spiritual capacities. W. H. Thorpe, *Science, Man and Morals* (London, 1965), and A. Comfort, *Nature and Human Nature* (Harmondsworth, 1969),* offer sharply contrasting views. Of the numerous books on problems of religious language, J. Macquarrie's *God-Talk* (London, 1967),* is particularly clear. F. P. Ferré, *Language, Logic and God* (London, 1970),* is also worth studying. A classic example of early twentieth-century liberal theology at work is A. Harnack's book of lectures, *What is Christianity?* (London, 1957).*

2 – The Validity of Conservatism

For a formal repudiation of 'liberalism', Cardinal Newman's

Apologia pro Vita Sua, especially Note A in the edition of 1886 (World Classics Edition, London, 1964), should be read. Liberalism, in the shape of a very moderate group of Anglican essays edited by B. H. Streeter, *Foundations* (London, 1912), is rebutted by R. A. Knox, *Some Loose Stones* (London, 1914). History seems to repeat itself in A. R. Vidler (ed), *Soundings* (Cambridge, 1962),* rebutted by E. L. Mascall, *Up and Down in Adria* (London, 1964).* Karl Barth's protest against continental liberal theology, first published in 1928, is most vigorously expressed in his *Word of God and Word of Man* (New York, 1957)*; of which Britain produced a paler expression in D. R. Davies, *On to Orthodoxy* (London, 1939), an influential pre-war book improbably connecting liberalism with Nazism.

3 – Pluriformity and the Essence of Christianity

J. H. Hick, *Christianity at the Centre* (London, 1968),* and J. Bowden, *Who is a Christian?* (London, 1970)* hover on the brink of asking what makes Christianity Christianity. Otherwise, in case the reader does not already know, evidence of the great variety of modern theology is found in the review books, H. R. Mackintosh, *Types of Modern Theology* (London, 1964),* a reprinted work which is by modern standards rather misleading on nineteenth century Germany, H. Zahrnt, *The Question of God* (London, 1969), an expertly written account of twentieth-century German Protestantism, and W. Nicholls, *Systematic and Philosophical Theology* (Harmondsworth, 1969).* For further study, V. A. Harvey, *The Historian and the Believer* (London, 1967),* probes the problem of Christianity's engagement with history.

4 – Objections to Christianity

L. Paul, *Alternatives to Christian Belief* (London, 1967), usefully surveys the modern search for meaning in the world outside Christianity. D. L. Edwards, *Religion and Change* (London, 1969),* is a sustained apologia for Christian faith in the face of contemporary challenges. A. T. Welford, *Christianity: A Psychologist's Translation* (London, 1971),* views Christianity from the standpoint of current psychological research and presents clearly a personal interpretation of it. Why the Churches failed in Nazi Germany is analysed by J. S. Conway, *The Nazi Persecution of the Churches* (London, 1968); a fascinating study of a Catholic's resistance is in G. Zahn, *Franz Jägerstätter, In Solitary Witness* (London, 1966). Dietrich Bonhoeffer's life is presented briefly in E. H. Robinson's biography (London, 1966);* delightfully and at greater length in M. Bosanquet, *The Life and Death of Dietrich Bonhoeffer* (London, 1968)* and with the full documentation in E. Bethge's authoritative study, *Dietrich Bonhoeffer* (London, 1970).

5 – Jesus and the Witness to Jesus
W. D. Davies, *Invitation to the New Testament* (London, 1967), is a balanced and well-written introduction. Of the many books on Jesus—it is advisable to read more than one—R. Bultmann, *Jesus and the Word* (London, 1958),* is a radical Protestant study; X. Leon-Dufour, *The Gospels and the Jesus of History* (London, 1968),* is a well-written Catholic book; and C. H. Dodd, *The Founder of Christianity* (London, 1971), is a typically lucid study from an eminent British biblical scholar. Recent writing on the resurrection includes C. F. Evans, *Resurrection and the New Testament* (London, 1970),* a detailed and important book arguing that there are many views of Christ's resurrection in the New Testament.

6 – Creation and God
L. C. Birch, *Nature and God* (London, 1965),* is by a scientist, A. Farrer, *A Science of God?* (London, 1966),* by a theo-

logian—both small, but valuable books. I. G. Barbour (ed), *Science and Religion* (London, 1968),* has collected together some recent writing on the perennial topic, and for those who think that it is all easy to reconcile, J. S. Hapgood's essay in *Soundings* (see Bibliography for Ch. 2), 'The Uneasy Truce between Science and Theology', would be a healthy jolt. As a guide to the obscurities of Teilhard de Chardin, N. M. Wildiers, *An Introduction to Teilhard de Chardin* (London, 1965),* is helpful.

7 – 'Other Religions' and Christianity

From the Christian end, P. Tillich, *Christianity and the Encounter of the World Religions* (London, 1963), L. Newbigin, *The Finality of Christ* (London, 1969),* and C. Davis, *Christ and the World Religions* (London, 1970), are recent examples of openness and concern. The professional approach to the phenomenon of religion is well exemplified in W. Cantwell Smith, *The Meaning and End of Religion* (New York, 1964). See the footnotes for other reading.

8 – The Essence of Christianity

What is outlined in this chapter is, in effect, a series of section headings for a systematic theology. Every writer differs in his presentation of the material, as would become clear from a glance at the chapter headings of the following large books: J. Macquarrie, *Principles of Christian Theology* (London, 1966),* G. D. Kaufman, *Systematic Theology* (New York, 1968), and J. A. Baker, *The Foolishness of God* (London, 1970). Macquarrie is existentialist, Kaufman historicist and Baker biblical in fundamental outlook. For myself I have learnt most from Friedrich Schleiermacher, the so-called 'father of modern theology', as would be clear from the chapter headings of his *Brief Outline on the Study of Theology* (Richmond,

Virginia, 1966),* tr. T. N. Tice. See my introduction to his
life and thought in the 'Makers of Contemporary Theology'
series (London, 1971).*

(*Indicates that the book is in paperback or limp covers.)